SELFLESS CHOICES

SELFLESS CHOICES

A MOTHER'S DETERMINED PURSUIT TO EDUCATE HER SON

SHARON R. YOUNG

Printed in the United States of America.

ISBN: 979-89864039-0-8 Trade Paperback
ISBN: 979-8-9864039-1-5 eBook

Library of Congress Control Number: 2022914389

First printing, 2022.

Cover and interior design by Glen Edelstein, Hudson Valley Book Design

To Marsha K. Moore, my biggest motivator and supporter. I could not have completed this book without your dedication to edit and offer intuitive feedback.

My son, one of the smartest, unassuming, and gentle spirited people I know, who welcomed the idea when I expressed a desire to tell our story. You are my love and inspiration.

CONTENTS

INTRODUCTION

For each generation, there are innumerable justice issues that people of color need to address on behalf of themselves and others. Personally the justice issue I have chosen to focus on is ensuring that people of color have access to adequate education options. This focus was inspired by my own lived experiences, and I now make it a priority to alert and invite forward those impacted by these inequitable systems . . . Some years ago, when my child was approaching school age, I realized I was not the only parent out on a limb questioning the inner-city public school system or the public school system in general, with all of its pitfalls and the lack funds to provide for the children. Rather than sit still I actively sought solutions.

In the late 1990s, when my son left for boarding school, I started writing to fill a deep void in my soul. I had just lost daily interaction with the most important person in my life—he was now in a different state and miles away. At that time, my putting pen to paper was in no way altruistic; rather, it sprang from a need to comfort myself, perhaps even to help soothe my fears, my anxieties, my doubts, and, sometimes, my shame.

Writing was therapeutic. It helped to displace some of my unhappiness. I was often reminded of my recent life change by family, friends, and, sometimes, random individuals I met on subway cars or park benches, with whom I shared my woes. As some listened, they expressed concern that after my son graduated from boarding high school, I might as well say "goodbye," because he would more than likely go off to college and, thereafter, make his home elsewhere, as so many young college graduates do.

Over the years, I periodically picked up the almost-completed written manuscript. I was immensely proud of myself for having stockpiled an abundance of material from the schools (both middle and high), and an interesting and arresting idea surfaced and began to grow. Perhaps these gems could be shared in more than just passing conversations.

I began evaluating the accumulation with a new level of intensity. The collection included notes, letters, brochures, and literature with documented timelines from which I could draw in order to tell this story. I have provided keys to discovering some critically essential features of the independent school experience, particularly through the eyes of a woman of color, an African American/Latino.

While this material was collected some years ago, my *current* research reveals that not much has changed. Many public schools are primarily the same, with some inner-city schools more inadequate than in past years. The independent private schools are primarily the same, apart from the tuition increases.

Further, the application, testing, and financial aid processes remain unchanged, except for a few tweaks here and there, given the advances in technology with newer and more widely used software.

Because I had written much of the manuscript some time ago (excluding up-to-date detailed information and the "Helpful Organizations and Websites" section), it was easier for me to put the facts in an orderly sequence as I utilized the literature in my possession; otherwise, it would have been extremely challenging for me to draw from memory only.

Periodically, as I read through the manuscript, I would occasionally add and delete, and, for several years, I did nothing. The manuscript stayed in a file on my computer, and a hard copy lay in a desk drawer.

With time, I have learned that when one writes, rereading and rewriting events from the past (and sometimes the present), the dredged-up feelings are not always favorable. The writing process can bring up a good number of uncomfortable emotions, which might be disguised or manifested by over-eating, indulging in too many glasses of cabernet sauvignon, or just plain moping. As Mary Karr humorously points out in her book *The Art of Memoir*, "Every memoirist I know seems doomed to explore the past in an often-agonized death march down the pages." The more I wrote, however, the more it became clear that I had to put those uncomfortable feelings aside. A new priority had been defined. I had knowledge gained from my experiences and firsthand resources in my possession that I felt compelled to impart to countless young parents/grandparents who were at a loss. Some may feel as though they are at the mercy of our public school educational system. Many may question whether they should relocate to have access to better school districts. And others may question whether they should go against the status quo of the schools their children attend and make sufficient inquiries to warrant evidential change. Not to be discouraging, but please be aware that beneficial change takes time. Yet change is necessary and must start somewhere; it may as well start with you! I am a firm believer in "If you think you can't, you won't. And you sure as heck won't try." I am hopeful that this book will, at the very least, ignite the beginning of a long-awaited conversation.

Independent private boarding school availability for African Americans living in the South is not a new concept. In the 1800s and 1900s, many children of color had to travel great distances to have access to an education. The other alternative was for parents to send their children North to live with relatives and thus attend integrated, predominately white schools. Because of these and other factors, Black-owned boarding schools were developed. Boarding schools for some African American families, especially the more elite, became the answer at that time; several opened their doors but have since closed. The Palmer Memorial Institute boarding school in North Carolina was one of the most well-known and prestigious preparatory schools of its kind. Founder Dr. Charlotte Hawkins Brown welcomed more than 1,000 African American students over the years before the school's doors closed. By the mid sixties to early seventies, some Black families did not consider public or independent private day schools; instead, they sent their high school–aged children to such white independent private boarding schools as Groton and Phillips Exeter. That said, enrollment for many Black-owned boarding schools declined, resulting in more closures.

Today, because Black-owned boarding schools are few, considering the entire scope of the independent private school industry, the choices are few as well. Since our family did not have a history of applying to or attending these independent boarding schools, I had little to draw from. However, had we known any existed during the time of our son's eligibility, a Black-owned boarding school certainly would have been a consideration. *It should be pointed out that the schools (day or boarding) that our son did attend provided him with an excellent education. No complaints in that department!*

Independent private schools offer one of the most comprehensive educational experiences any caring parent could dream of for their child. Our personal story adds a bit of flavor to the journey taken, thereby outlining what a family can expect from such an experience should they decide to pursue this route.

Since the onset of the coronavirus pandemic, public school teachers have been retiring at higher-than-normal rates. To make matters more complicated, not many people are going into the teaching profession, largely due to the lack of respect some public schoolteachers receive. This, coupled with the fact that there is already a shortage of teachers, has made for a rather serious problem. We appear to just hope that over time this situation will resolve itself. There are solutions, but we must become more creative in finding them. Public school teachers are just as important and necessary as private school teachers, who, like their students, enjoy a privileged work environment. For example, private school teachers probably never have to face a lack of funding for supplies, or endure overcrowded classrooms, or tolerate poorly ventilated or heated/cooled school buildings. These three things begin the list of inadequacies facing many public schools, all of which can make it increasingly difficult to teach. We need dedicated teachers! They are influential and have changed the lives of millions, oftentimes seeing in us what we do not see in ourselves. Teachers are all-important to our nation and the growth of our children.

We live in a fast-paced, get-to-the-point society! For that purpose, as well as others, I have made this book an easy read. The reader should be able to dive right into what is important for their given situation.

This is both a *memoir* and a *how-to* book. It depicts actual events and reflects the author's present recollection of events over a period of time. I have told the story as candidly as I can. It has been important to me to protect the identity and privacy of individuals involved, therefore, for this reason, some names have been changed.

I have provided references and other resources as a convenience to the reader; they are not to imply endorsements.

I wish all of you the best on your journey!

1.

FEAR . . . OVERRULED

Start where you are. Use what you have.
Do what you can.
—Arthur Ashe

After a weekend visit to the St. Andrew's School in Delaware, where my son, Brad, was a student, I parked the car and was already mentally preparing myself for the next trip there in a few weeks. During the three-and-a-half-hour drive, I had reflected on the number of times I had gone to St. Andrew's . . . including the numerous visits prior to Brad's first day there, parents weekend, arts expo, and sports competitions, not to mention the *"Here I am, I just miss you!"* visits. As exhausted as I was on that crisp fall afternoon, my thoughts were racing with anticipation. I was determined to start a project that I felt was long overdue: to write an informative book on a subject that needed to be explored, to tell my story—our story. In doing so, I hoped to provide other parents the motivation they would need to get actively involved in their children's education and to either learn of or seek out available alternatives.

Over a period of time, I had begun to stockpile literature from both Brad's middle and high schools, so I started there. I read as much information as I could on the school systems—both public and private—in my region. I had a background as a persistent advocate for education, and a strong intuition regarding the sacrifices and commitments one must make to oversee the education of their child, so I felt I had an obligation to impart what I knew to parents/grandparents who were perhaps less informed than I or who were questioning their rights with regard to the public school system. More specifically, I wanted this information to reach the parents whose children were being underserved in their current educational setting, along with those who believed their hands were tied with few or no alternatives when it came to their children's education, whether their children were attending traditional public schools or other institutions.

Even as the desire to begin writing overcame me that afternoon, equally strong feelings crept in as they had from time to time delaying my attempts. Unfortunately, with so many other demands on my time—a challenging job and family obligations (including an aging mother, aunt, and uncle)—little room was left to explore any form of creativity. Further, in hindsight, I wondered about all the wasted time and energy I spent while in solitude, not wanting to do anything but just sit, think, and contemplate whether I had made the right choice to send my son to a boarding preparatory high school in Delaware. This was, in fact, a kind of internal punishment. I missed him terribly. While my rational mind said, "Yes, it's okay; he will benefit from the academic experience," my motherly instincts voiced the contrary. To add to my dilemma, many of my family members and friends looked at me with a jaundiced eye, implying their disapproval. "Why on earth would you do something like that? Boarding schools are for rich white trust fund kids whose parents have little time to spend with them. Not *our* kids." Whether their misconceptions were openly implied or spoken, their words lay heavily on my mind.

Nevertheless, my apprehension putting pen to paper also stemmed from my fear of writing. Did I have the staying power to complete this writing project? More importantly, was I comfortable writing something as lengthy as a book?

I had always been uncomfortable with writing . . . short pieces, long ones, or those in between. And although I was a college graduate and what one would consider a "professional," I felt that the inner-city public school system had failed me in many ways, as it had so many millions of adults and children throughout the United States.

Throughout the years, I have witnessed many professionals and young adults who have found writing to be a challenge. The thoughts were there, the ideas were there, and, for the most part, the critical thinking was there, but putting those thoughts on paper was a slightly different story. The fear associated with writing well paralyzed so many of us. I have often questioned a society that would allow a school system to fail to arm its children with something so important and powerful as the written word.

2.

A HIGH SCHOOL GRADUATE— THE GOAL THEN

Obstacles are those frightful things you see when
you take your eyes off your goal.
—Henry Ford

Growing up, I'd had no choice but to attend a New York inner-city public school, beginning with P.S. 157 in Harlem and continuing on to James Monroe High School in the Bronx. Back in the sixties and seventies, education in the inner-city public schools provided what one might consider a slightly better teaching environment than today, if only for the mere fact that Blacks and other minority children who attended these schools were oftentimes integrated with white children and, therefore, had the same academic exposure. Also, during that time, I think our parents—most of whom were first-generation southerners, Caribbean Islanders, or Latinos—were more concerned with their children completing high school and not as concerned with questioning the quality of the education the public schools offered. A high school graduate, that was the goal . . . college was a bonus. As far as our parents knew, we were getting a good education.

Our generation of parents may not have completed high school or sought a college degree. My mother, for example, who was from Georgia, completed her high school education—I continue to treasure her beautiful smile in the photo of her wearing her cap and gown—but did not obtain a degree when she later attended Bronx Community College, well after my brother and I became teenagers. As with many southerners, especially the middle-class southerners, education was highly emphasized, with most attending traditional Black colleges like Spelman, Howard, and Morehouse, to name a few. My dad, on the other hand, a Cuban American born in Tampa, Florida, left high school to join the navy, even though he was a very bright individual and an aspiring songwriter.

Education was somewhat emphasized in our household. I grew up during the sixties and seventies, when women were expected to find someone who would become a good husband and make a decent salary and marry him after completing high school, as opposed to seeking a college degree.

Unlike most of my female friends, I attended college directly after finishing high school. However, in order to maintain a decent average, I had to work a lot harder than some of the other students, many of whom were from out of state or had gone to public high schools in the suburbs. In essence, I was forced to play catch-up during those four years and well into my adulthood. I would find myself having to do many rewrites of correspondences, memos, etc., in the corporate world, which was frustrating and very time-consuming.

As it turned out, I did begin to write the weekend following my trip to St. Andrew's, and, as time went on, I wrote more and more; my anxieties began to slowly diminish.

3.

RECRUITMENT? DIVERSITY NIGHT

Don't judge each day by the harvest you reap
but by the seeds that you plant.
—Robert Louis Stevenson

I have had several discussions on the subject of school diversity
with my friend Alice, who, like me, had a child in one of the
private independent schools. We were aware that many of the
independent schools, both day and boarding, actively sought
to diversify their student population. This was quite evident
from the invitations we had received over the years to attend
"school diversity nights." Many of the schools would schedule
an evening during the school year for minority parents to
discuss diversity, which usually focused on the school's efforts
to make certain their *current* minority students felt comfortable.
"How can we better serve our minority students?" was usually
the unspoken theme. In the schools' efforts to raise the comfort
level of our children, a small percentage of the discussion
focused on recruitment efforts to bring more minority students
to independent schools.

I actually wondered at times to what extent the schools really wanted this diversity to take place. Did they choose not to disclose this information to a wider public for fear of having large numbers of minority children and their parents flock to their doorsteps? I am pleased to add, however, that *today*, many of the private independent schools have proactively developed a Diversity and Inclusion Department to assist in recruiting students of color.

On a different but similar thought, were there educators who could have suggested that parents search for an alternative to a public school education . . . perhaps an independent school? Or did the majority of public schoolteachers and administrators lack this information? Certainly, some of these educators may have gone to independent schools themselves or knew of friends or relatives who had. Or was there something with the inner-city public schools' administration and/ or faculty, who may have over the years witnessed many bright children but said nothing to the parents about the benefits of seeking a more challenging environment for children of their ability level?

In any event, the fact that independent schools exist appears to be relatively unknown in minority households, unless the families are among the elite. I often questioned why so many parents I have had discussions with over the years had never heard of independent schools. Almost without fail, when private schools were mentioned, their first thoughts were almost always of parochial or Catholic schools.

I am reminded of the day I received an autographed book, which not only enhanced my library but my life. *Black Ice*, written by Lorene Cary, captures beautifully and with candor her experiences as an African American student who pioneered an all-white independent private boarding school in New Hampshire in the early 1970s. Ms. Cary had visited St. Andrew's while Brad was a student there.

More recently, as I was cleaning out my bookshelves, I ran across the autographed copy of *Black Ice* inscribed to me; I immediately thought of the day when Brad had brought the book home with such pride . . . to give to me. He had been excited by Ms. Cary's visit to St. Andrew's as she talked about her new book, and she had apparently given special attention to him. I happily accepted the book and was especially moved by the inscription, as it read: *For Sharon, A gift from Brad, who made a warm welcome for me here at St. Andrew's. You must be so proud—All Best, Lorene Cary, 2001.*

I devoured the contents of the book right away, wanting to really feel the connection with someone who had survived the boarding school experience as a Black adolescent in the seventies. As I read, I, of course, kept in mind that her parents had made an emotional sacrifice so that Lorene, who was provided a scholarship, could have the best education possible, amidst the discrimination of those times. *Black Ice* told the story quite well and with relaxed humor. Lorene survived! She went on to become the author of several books, an educator, a social activist, and founder of the Art Sanctuary—giving voice to African American talent in the literary and performing arts arena.

4.

WHAT RESPONSIBILITIES AND RIGHTS DO YOU HAVE? QUESTIONS ANYONE?

Never give up, for that is just the place
and time that the tide will turn.
—Harriet Beecher Stowe

Some years ago, I was employed as a substitute teacher in a West Harlem middle school. Robert, who was a student in most of my classes, was in my opinion a bright young boy with an abundance of potential. The following year, he was scheduled to graduate to go on to high school. One day, out of curiosity, I asked Robert, "Has anyone in the school ever suggested that you look into other high schools besides Vanderbilt?" Vanderbilt was the nearby high school that most of his peers were going to attend.

"Yes," he nodded. "Bronx High School of Science, and Stuyvesant High School." I was thrilled to hear it. Both of those schools have very good reputations and were among New York City's most selective public high schools.

"That's great!" I replied. "What day is the test?"

"December 3rd," he answered.

Each year, a few thousand students line up for a chance to take this rigorous admissions exam. But, unfortunately, of the few thousand students who apply to the two schools, only a fraction are accepted. It is an extremely competitive process. Imagine a rejected student's disappointment after setting their sights on attending one of these schools and waiting a good part of the year to then learn they have been denied!

I was rooting for Robert, hoping he was not going to be one of the disappointed students. I also wondered why Robert's parents were not informed about possible alternatives, as a safety measure, just in case he was not accepted to either of these schools. It is good to be confident and assured, but, in my estimation, it is also good to have a back-up plan, especially on an issue as important as this one. While my stay as a sub at this particular middle school was brief, I asked Robert several times to have his mother contact me. She never did.

There is no doubt that the inner-city public schools can be very disruptive, with a great deal of distraction for those students who want to learn, as I had witnessed daily while subbing. When I hear or read statements similar to, "If you can't save them all, at least save as many as you can," I think of Robert. I also think of a movie I once watched some years ago titled *Lean on Me*. Based on a true story and produced sometime in the late eighties, it stirred a great deal of controversy among parents of school-age children. The movie portrayed a recently appointed principal of an inner-city public high school who, at the risk of possibly losing his job, was forced to make a major decision. The principal was keenly aware of how difficult it was for children to learn in a disruptive environment. So, he had to decide whether to allow a group of students who were disruptive and had given up on learning to negatively influence those students who still wanted to learn. Despite opposition from the school board, some of the teaching staff, and the parents of the children with "behavioral problems," the principal maintained his ground, and the disruptive kids were given a deadline to leave. The parents of the disruptive group of children unfortunately showed their displeasure at having their children removed from the school by taking action in the "eleventh hour," all to no avail. Although forewarned, they only seemed to acknowledge that their children had problems when it was too late to reverse the principal's decision. Many of these children were now nearing the school age limit, having been held back several times over. Where were they to go but to the streets? No other school would accept them. They were now labeled as menaces to the school and perhaps, over time, to society.

Disturbingly, situations similar to this happen all the time. Either the kids drop out on their own or they are forced to leave because of numerous, sometimes violent, disturbances, or they've reached the school age limit after being held back so many times.

Although the movie was fiction, much of it mimicked real life. Who is to say that five or six out of the group of kids that was asked to leave the school could not have excelled, had their energies been properly channeled at an early age? They may have made a notable and positive impact on society, perhaps becoming entrepreneurs or inventors of some sort, or developing a cure for a life-threatening disease. We will never know, will we? As in the movie, similar situations frequently happen in real life, where children drop out and have pretty much given up on productive learning.

"A mind is a terrible thing to waste" is one of the most profound and memorable statements ever developed for an education ad campaign. Think about it. There are so many bright children in a minority group in the United States today, yet we as parents do not always put forth the necessary energy early enough or go that extra mile to ensure their success. Far too many adults often think that it is the responsibility of the schools to see to it that our children are properly educated; however, it is also *our* responsibility as parents to uncover our children's limitations and/or potential early on. For example, if a child needs special skills assistance—a child with a learning disability, or a child who is crying out for a challenging academic environment—we as parents need to be aware of this. A proactive approach on the part of the parent is surely needed in either situation.

In the epilogue of the book *Don't Blame the Kids*, Gene I. Maeroff writes:

> "What I hope I have made clear is that the quality of schools depends on adults, not kids. Young people are powerless in this drama, bit players on a stage on which their elders have all of the best parts. Most youngsters want desperately to succeed. No child ever entered first grade intending to join education's casualty list."

Additionally, Steve Perry, founder of the Capital Prep Magnet School in Hartford, Connecticut, commented on CNN, "There is no such thing as a strong community with a weak school system or a weak community with a strong school system. . . . When you have an area in which we have children failing as a standard, we can only expect that the grown people are not handling their business." It really is up to us.

What I hope to achieve with this book includes three key points, which will give the reader insight into the independent school experience and to help them understand that there are options from which to draw for their children's education. *One,* I will encourage parents to take time to recognize their children's potential and seek to place them on a path that will both challenge them and help them to develop their critical thinking skills. *Two,* I include what to look for when applying to an independent private school, along with step-by-step procedures on how to apply. *Three,* I address possible limitations, such as the fact that an independent school might be out of reach because of distance. Let's say the nearest independent *day* school is a two-hour drive away, and an independent *boarding* school is out of the question. The parent would do best to *not* remain complacent and take what's handed to them. Instead, they would be well-served to make enough purposeful noise to at least elicit change within the public school their child must attend.

Many people of color "are" and have been strategically pushed behind due to sheer discrimination. This is especially true in the education arena, which continues to be quite evident in our public school system and the manner in which education dollars are allocated. Access to a comprehensive education holds the keys to unleashing opportunities that can benefit all of humanity. When we discover or determine that our lives possess intrinsic value, we have arrived at a beautiful place. We need not apologize for seeking a "respectable" education, something we are all clearly eligible to receive. It's how we go about making this happen that will be the deciding factor. Remember, you must be diligent when it comes to your child's education.

*   *   *

As a child, I had a situation happen to me that could have been labeled as discrimination. This subject was not something that was openly discussed in the presence of children, at least not in our household. Our parents apparently shielded us from any perceived prejudices to the extent that I was not aware of such a concept until I started school in Harlem; I attended P.S. 157 (the building is now a condominium), where most of the teachers were white. One teacher consistently picked on me; her reasoning, I will never know. Too embarrassed or shy, I did not tell my mother. When the teacher suggested a meeting with my mother, my very best childhood friend made my mom aware that Ms. Dunbar always singled me out and picked on me. During the meeting, she indicated to my mother that I should join a Special Education class. My mother, who had volunteered in our school during my brother's second and third year, explained to the teacher that she was not in agreement and would not consider a Special Ed class placement. Also, my mother said that if the teacher insisted, she would take it further, possibly to the school board. Mom was mad, to say the least. She asked that I be removed from Ms. Dunbar's class and be placed with a different teacher. My mom was a quiet woman, and, having volunteered her time for two years, knew the ropes and the chain of command of the school system. I did well in the other class, and Special Ed was never discussed again.

Parents have rights; know them! This was in the early sixties. Today, there are guidelines in abundance to support families. I am not suggesting you march over to the school wanting to rip someone's head off. Today, most schools are willing to work with the parents. Get familiar with **FERPA**, the Family Educational Rights and Privacy Act. Had my mother followed that teacher's suggestion, I would not be sitting here writing this manuscript. Further, an old friend of mine, Beth, who is a few years younger than I, recently shared a story with me of her experience as one of the first and only children of color to be bused from the Jamaica section of Queens, New York, to what was to later become an integrated, diverse school in Woodside, Queens. Beth's parents went to great lengths to see to it that she was to attend that school. Beth, a first grader, said the teacher asked her, "Who is the current vice president?" She didn't know the answer but excelled in other reasoning areas; the teacher still asked that she be removed from the class. Beth's mother and father got involved, and she continued with her studies in that class until the end of the school year and remained at the school throughout her elementary years. Today Beth tells me that she received the best education at that Woodside school, and her reading was at a much higher level than that of her peers. She is one of the brightest people I know and is now a retired actuarial analyst.

As adults, we have a responsibility to those who came before us to forge ahead and secure an education for our children, that offers cultivation of skills and an outlet for the creativity that is uniquely ours. As this focused preparation is embraced, it provides the opportunity for one to successfully compete in a society, that has for so long forced people of color to hush, be quiet, and "keep it 'movin'."

A non-active, wait-and-see approach would almost assuredly be a disservice to the child, while being proactive may ensure the child's success, now and in the future. Know your rights as a parent and use your power!

Often, due to their own societal/cultural indoctrination, some parents may feel somewhat unsure as they question the competency of a school or demand changes, thinking that since the administration and faculty are professionals, surely, they must know best. However, your primal right as a parent is the right to ask questions.

There are specific **legal** and **federal** rights that you should be aware of:

1. You have the right to expect an appropriate all-inclusive education for your child.
2. You have the right to see your child's complete school record, including test scores, teacher comments, formal disciplinary actions, and counselors' notes. You have the right to be furnished with copies of all school documents. You also have the right to demand changes in the record that appear to be biased or incorrect.
3. You have the right to a written notice of any evaluations on your child. You have the right to attend teacher conferences in which your child and/or his test scores, school behavior, and academic performance are being discussed with other teachers, administrators, or counselors.
4. You have the right to notification of any atypical educational placement (temporary and

permanent) of your child, and you have the right
to appeal.

This list provides only a few of your parental rights. It is in
no way an exhaustive one. Please check online to read about the
Family Educational Rights and Privacy Act (FERPA)
for more information.

CHARTER SCHOOLS

Charter schools were slowly becoming a household word
during the time I was considering schools for Brad. While I
had heard about charter schools, I didn't have enough information about the program and how it worked. There had been
behind-the-scenes talk about the charter school concept, and I
vaguely knew of the grassroots model charter school located in
Minnesota. The question that has formed since then is, if I had
known more about the school at that time, what good would
that have done? We lived in New York.

Charter school law began in 1991 in the state of Minnesota.
The first charter school, called the City Academy, opened its
doors in 1992 in the city of St. Paul, Minnesota. By the year
2003, forty states, including Puerto Rico and the District of
Columbia, were signed into law, and more charter schools
began to open.

In 1992, St. Paul's City Academy Charter School sought to
recruit low-income and disadvantaged students. The school's
model was predicated on recruiting students who were dropouts
living in substance abuse environments and/or poverty-stricken

homes. At least one-quarter of the students were considered homeless.

Later, the school's model focused more on those students who had unsuccessful experiences at traditional and alternative schools and had fallen through the cracks.

The academy stressed two themes, "Respect" and "Life Lessons." Students agreed to and were bound by a contract, which determined what, as well as when, the contract would be fulfilled. For example, for a student who had committed to providing a community service, fulfilling that commitment would be the goal; another student might make a commitment of when and how they would prepare to obtain a driver's license.

Initially, students ranged in age from 13–19; over a period of time, the school has raised the enrollment age to 15–21, realizing that some students may need more time to complete the program. One positive that is noteworthy is that the school has a low attrition rate, with students determined to see their commitment through. Small class sizes are still maintained, although the school has expanded in student population.

Like most charter schools, City Academy was sponsored by the public school system and publicly funded, along with some private funding from the College of St. Catherine. This first model charter school has struggled over the years with low proficiency rates in math or science, despite its low attrition rate.

Today many charter schools are founded by educators, community leaders, or, at times, parents. Some are privately funded, as well as publicly funded by federal and state dollars, therefore, tuition is free. The curriculum is overseen by the public school system. The charter school concept has broadened over the years, and its demand serves as a catalyst for expansion.

Having more parents interested has made it necessary for some charter schools to develop a lottery system for admissions, especially in the urban and more densely populated areas. Some parents may view the lottery system as a challenge. Yes, it can be daunting and viewed as a hit or miss, or even as a shot in the dark. But it surely is worth investigating. If a parent is interested, it is always advisable to seek enrollment in the lower grades—usually there are more spots open, and once a sibling is admitted, the schools will many times opt to give priority to the other sibling(s) in the lottery process.

Just as traditional public schools are not all the same, neither are charter schools. There are many successful charter schools throughout the country; finding them just takes a little investigation on the part of the parent. One successful example is a system of schools in the Bridgeport, Connecticut, and NYC area called the Capital Preparatory Harbor Charter Schools, founded by Dr. Steve Perry, visionary, and former principal. The first in its model, a preparatory *magnet* school, was implemented in 2005; it has nurtured and sent 100 percent of its predominately low-income students on to become college graduates.

Dr. Perry, who I greatly admire, saw a need to start a charter school after a parent approached him and asked, "Why is it that the wealthy get to go to the best schools?" That simple statement resonated with him, and by the year 2014, the first Capital Preparatory Harbor Charter School was developed. Because of high demand, 2,700 students had applied for the *only* fifty seats that were available. The charter school opened its doors in 2015 in Bridgeport, serving grades seven through twelve, and it later added an elementary school in the fall of

2017. The charter school branched out in 2017 to open the Capital Preparatory Harlem Charter School, with the financial assistance of media mogul Mr. Sean "Diddy" Combs. Another Capital Preparatory School recently opened its doors in the Bronx, New York, area. With each expansion, thousands of students continue to apply. The school seeks to build a core to create a culture of respect and empathy within and throughout all aspects of the community. Their mission statement reads, "The mission of Capital Preparatory Schools is to provide historically disadvantaged students with the college and career readiness skills needed to become responsible and engaged citizens for social justice."

Charter school curriculums and statewide testing are overseen by the public school system. And although the schools are independently run and have autonomy in curriculum and staffing, they are held accountable to state academic standards— with the expectation of a high-quality education for all of its students. Most charter schools offer smaller class sizes and a family atmosphere, where students and teachers are open to trying new things beyond what may typically occur in the traditional public schools. So, they are free to do what works. Charters attract highly qualified, certified teachers.

Additional charter schools are needed. If more philan-thropists, other wealth groups, sports icons, and entertainers like Mr. Combs knew and embraced the need, perhaps more charter schools would soon be in the making. Just a thought!

To locate a charter school near you, go directly to the school's website to find out their criteria for admissions or visit niche.com, which is an invaluable resource when searching for a school. Niche is discussed briefly in chapter 24.

5.

LIFE CHALLENGES? YES! BUT IT'S TIME TO BEGIN KINDERGARTEN

Challenges are what make life interesting and overcoming them is what makes life meaningful.
—Joshua J. Marine

My own journey had not been an easy one. In addition to the challenges associated with being a newly divorced parent—coping with the emotional trauma and raising a child as the custodial parent—I was driven to search for a variety of avenues through which to educate our son, Brad. We lived in the Bronx during that time, which meant that Brad, who was about four, was destined to attend one of the neighboring inner-city public schools. The development we lived in was huge, and, to some extent, overpopulated. The two public schools in the surrounding area were overcrowded, and in my estimation would not offer the quality of education I expected for Brad. Shortly after my ex-husband, Al, and I separated, I had considered moving out of the city, and possibly out of the state, to search for a better life and education for Brad. I envisioned suburban living, where the schools were comparatively better.

As a way of coping with the divorce, I began to visit several cities where a few of our relatives lived. Minneapolis was in one of the few states where relatives did not live, yet I fell in love with it and strongly considered moving there. However, I remained cognizant of the fact that if we moved out of state, Brad would have limited access to Al. So, after this reality set in, leaving the state was no longer a consideration, and the immediate outcome led us to remain in the Bronx and search for a nearby school for kindergarten.

Employed in Manhattan at the time, I had briefly considered moving to the suburbs of New York, perhaps Rockland, Orange, or upper Westchester County. The commute to any of those counties could take at least an hour or an hour and a half, and I feared what would happen in case of a medical emergency. Would someone be there to help should something happen?

Brad attended a preschool sponsored by the local YMCA during that time. When Al and I had been together, I didn't have to worry about Brad being picked up. Al worked in the South Bronx at the time and had gladly taken on this responsibility. Now, with him gone, I had to make certain Brad was picked up on time.

My mother, who had not yet retired and was still employed as a paraprofessional in one of the Bronx schools, continued to be supportive and helped when she could. Although she had a car and was in closer proximity to Brad's school than I was, to solely rely on her was unfair. There were lots of days when

I was running late because of the usual New York traffic and I would ask, "Mom, can you pick up Brad for me? I don't think I can get there in time." My mother was always accommodating and never complained; whatever she was doing, she dropped it to pick up her grandson.

The decision to move created such a dilemma for me that I did nothing. We just stayed! We continued to live in our Parkchester apartment in the Bronx. As it was, I was barely making it on time living close by; the idea of trying to get to Brad, given a much longer commute and having one less person there as a backup, seemed impossible. Still, with our nearby public schools leaving a lot to be desired—and the surrounding parochial schools not much better—I continued my search for schools.

6.

MAKE THE APPOINTMENT— REGISTER FOR THE ERB

Courage is the discovery that you may not win,
and trying when you know you can lose.
—*Tom Krause*

At the time, I knew very little about independent schools, the admissions process, or how to go about applying, except I was aware that Brad's brother, Parker, and sister, Hannah—both from Al's previous marriage—were attending or had attended the George School, an independent boarding high school located in Pennsylvania. I also knew that Alice's son, Santiago, who was slightly older than Brad, had recently entered the first grade at a midtown Manhattan independent school.

I had assumed that the tuition for these schools would cost an arm and a leg, yet I never bothered to ask Alice any detailed questions. When I did ask, Alice, who had apparently done her homework, she put my anxieties to rest by assuring me that many of the schools had fairly large endowments to assist with the tuition. With this in mind, she encouraged me to contact the Parents League of New York to obtain a booklet listing the local independent private schools and other relevant information. She also suggested that Brad take the Educational Records Bureau (ERB) test, which begins the process for admissions to the schools.

After receiving several brochures from a variety of schools and visiting three, I registered Brad for the ERB test for admission to kindergarten. We also began the rather lengthy application process. Please note, whereas when we were considering Brad's entrance to kindergarten the ERB test was given at their *then* testing site in Manhattan, *now* the individual private schools are responsible for administering assessment tests for those entering kindergarten and first grade.

The ERB prepares tests for grades second through twelve. Individuals can test at home or at a proctor site. Parents were—and still are—cautioned not to hire tutors for the test, as the ERB sees this practice as a disservice to a young child. They believe that the testing process should be of a relaxed manner so as not to distort the scoring, which can lead to inappropriate placement and could ultimately put a student under undue pressure to perform in the school in which they are placed.

The ERB testing center is a nonprofit organization that, at the time (in the late 1980s), provided assessment services to approximately 1,400 independent and select public schools. It now serves over 2,000 schools nationwide. The scoring of the test is based on developmental standards using the national population in a given age group. The combined headquarters and testing site at that time was located on East 42nd Street near Grand Central station in New York City. Now the administrative office is located on Park Avenue South

As Brad and I walked into the testing center, I took notice of the attractive waiting area with its dark, mahogany-trimmed windows, which complemented the striking white walls displaying brightly colored abstract paintings. We were greeted with a smile by the young receptionist, who reminded us that we were early. She continued typing, shifting her head toward us as she spoke. The busy phones, which seemingly rang every twenty seconds, interrupted our conversation. "Educational Records Bureau, may I help you?"

"Mrs. Young would you and Brad make yourselves comfortable and fill out these forms? When you're finished, please bring them back up to the desk. Thank you."

There were other parents, their children ranging in age, sitting expectantly in the waiting area. The children were called on one by one for testing. Brad was one of the last to be called; when his turn came, he eagerly departed from my side, taking the hand of the tester.

A child of four years old, Brad was a fearless, friendly boy who liked people; he was always ready to bond. I sometimes worried that if I did not keep close tabs on him, he would take the hand of a stranger and just walk off—thinking, of course, that he would be returned to me.

The test lasted about an hour and a half. Afterward, as we were preparing to leave, one of the test administrators who happened to be walking through the sitting area casually asked Brad, "How was it?" as he glanced at me. Brad, the talker that he was, nodded and commented on an area of the test that he apparently thought was a game of some kind. The administrator smiled; turning to me, he asked, "Which schools do you plan to apply to?"

I replied, "The Bank Street School."

A look of concern came over the administrator's face as

he said we should also consider applying to some of the other independent schools in the city, but he did not specify. I guess in his position he could not recommend any particular school.

I gathered Brad's sweater, coat, and other belongings while nervously eyeing him as he moved across the room. I smiled and repeatedly nodded in response to the administrator, not bothering to go into any further dialogue or to ask why he recommended we submit additional applications.

We left and went on about our day. As unprepared as I was for that slight bit of unsettling information from the administrator and the slow midday subway ride home, I summoned up enough energy to do a load of laundry, write out some bills, and prep for dinner, while Brad played with his toys in his room. As the only child in the household, Brad appeared to enjoy his many toys and gadgets. As he played, he would talk with himself, laugh with himself, and sometimes talk to Abe, his Cabbage Patch friend. Thinking back, I sometimes wonder how lonely that must have been for him. At least I had had my brother, whom I loved dearly and who was a year older than I, to look forward to daily interactions with . . . even if those interactions were mostly squabbles.

*   *   *

Brad scored well on the ERB test. About a month later, I received a letter from the Bank Street School's admissions office. Brad had not been accepted for their kindergarten class. I was very disappointed. Al, who had been relatively involved in the school-visiting process, was also disappointed. I telephoned my mother to tell her the bad news and to get moral support. I said nothing to Brad about it.

"Hi, Mom."

"What's wrong with you?" She had a knack for knowing when something was wrong.

"Oh, nothing." I paused. "I can't believe Brad was not accepted to the Bank Street School!" I blurted.

"What? He did so well on that test!" she said. "You mean the ERB test, right? Yes, what are you going to do?"

"I don't know. Can I call you later?"

I was so upset, I just wanted to lie down.

Later in the day, I called Alice to share the context of the letter, who also indicated that we should have applied to more than one school. I recalled my brief conversation with the administrator at the ERB testing center and was annoyed with myself; I had been so enamored with the Bank Street School after our visit there that I had neglected to consider following Alice's and the administrator's suggestion to apply to a variety of independent schools. We could have at least applied to the other two schools we had visited in addition to the Bank Street School, where the competition was extreme. After all, it was one of the notably well-known schools in the area. I discovered the hard way that applying to only one school was not the best decision.

Beginning the application process at the kindergarten and first-grade level is very competitive. Some of the wealthiest people in the country send their children to these schools, with many deciding very early on which schools their children will attend. The competition is fierce! There are too many applicants and not enough spots. Regrets about not applying to a variety of schools bothered me for some time.

For the wealthy, financing their children's education may not be a problem. However, I would advise families who are relying on school funding to assist with tuition to also consider a variety of schools during the application process for both acceptance purposes and the financial aspect.

7.

THE RACE IS ON!

The will to win, the desire to succeed, the urge to reach
your full potential . . . these are the keys that will unlock
the door to personal excellence.
—Confucius

Having Brad attend one of the surrounding public schools was going to be difficult, so I half-heartedly began looking into parochial schools. Both Brad and I were baptized as Catholics but did not follow the traditions, except for an occasional Mass service. During our visits to parochial schools, I noticed that the physical environment of both the schools and the staff appeared somewhat stoic. Also, for all three of the surrounding parochial schools we visited, the kindergarten classes ended their days at 11:30 a.m. This meant that I would have to find a reliable person to pick Brad up from school each day.

Late April had rolled around, and time was passing. I continued my research, made phone calls, and had talks with colleagues and with other parents. Locating a good school was my mission.

One afternoon, I decided to call our local school district office. I had been placed on hold for more than twenty minutes when a very kind and seemingly patient voice informed me of the "Exceptionally Gifted Program" located within District 11. The person, who later introduced herself as Ms. Gallop, indicated that there were a series of tests to be taken for this program: the Otis-Lennon School Ability Test and the Stanford-Binet IQ test. The Otis-Lennon (a screening test) was scheduled to be administered a week later. Although we were late in signing up, Ms. Gallop said she would squeeze us in for an appointment. I was extremely grateful, thanking her repeatedly until we ended the call.

Both tests are used to assess a child's intellectual ability. The Otis-Lennon is visual, both pictorial and figural, which assesses verbal reasoning and comprehension. The Stanford-Binet tests one's IQ. If a child does well on the Otis-Lennon test, they are then referred to the Stanford-Binet test.

Based on my knowledge of Brad's abilities and how I had seen him interact with other children his age, I had confidence that he could pass both tests and qualify for the program.

*　　*　　*

Somewhat perplexed by the term "gifted child," I decided to do a little research. I came across a book published in 1981, written by an educator and mother of a "gifted child." As she explained it, every child has a gift: a memory for faces, an extraordinary love of music, a memory for specific facts, a genius for manipulating numbers, the ability to kick a soccer ball, or an infectious smile. Every child is a gifted child. However, there are children with mental and physical abilities far beyond those of others in a similar age category. They're usually quicker than most, more energetic, more inquisitive, a bit of a mystery, and precocious.

According to the Columbus Group, "Giftedness is asynchronous development in which advanced cognitive abilities and heightened intensity combine to create inner experiences and awareness that are qualitatively different from the norm. That asynchrony increases with higher intellectual capacity. The uniqueness of the gifted renders them particularly vulnerable and requires modification in parenting, teaching, and counseling in order to develop optimally."

As gifted children age, they are usually labeled as eggheads, nerds, high achievers, and exceptional learners. In the classroom, their behavior is more often than not misinterpreted, while underachievement is mistaken for low ability. Creative wit is considered a lack of respect. Restlessness is viewed as a need for discipline. The writer gives an example of a misunderstood gifted child:

Carl, at age five, could march into a room and take over. "What are those things on your desk? What are you doing? How come you're doing that now? Do you have any gum? What day is this? That's in the wrong place; it should be over there!"

Most adults took an instant dislike to him. He asked too many questions. As far as they were concerned, he had no self-control. But Carl was intelligently gifted. And when given a challenging project, he would work tirelessly until it was completed.

The tragedy is that children, like Carl, if not placed in the proper environment, are often damaged by the educational system. Without an educational system that keeps pace with a gifted child's ability to quickly absorb a large amount of material, and without the necessary emotional support, the gifted child at best can fail, and at worst exhibit conduct which can result in disruptive behavior and disciplinary action. Failure and low self-esteem may turn their gifts to negative and destructive pursuits.

As educators came to better understand the needs and the struggles of gifted children, special programs were set up within the public school system to accommodate these children. The most widely known program at that time was the Talented and Gifted (TAG) program. Later, the Exceptionally Gifted Program was developed.

More recently, books were written by authors Angela Wayning *Giftedness*, and Karen Andersen, *Gifted Children* each covering the subject of gifted children, further exploring the characteristics of these children as well as the challenges many face throughout their lives. For example, during the gifted child's early years, bullying can be a real problem which can contribute to serious consequences later.

When a gifted child is bullied by other children, it is often because of the gifted child's scholastic strengths, and it may cause the child to hide their "giftedness." Gifted children may struggle with why this is happening to them and try to take on the responsibility of how to make it stop. This can be true for *any* child who is bullied, but especially the gifted child who is deemed more emotional and sensitive to his environment and this kind of threat. They may, as a result, become embarrassed by their academic gifts, be more self-critical, and therefore develop a lack of interest in school, or they may become a perfectionist to a fault. These traits may stay with them throughout their adulthood.

Both teachers and parents need to assume a position of support to circumvent bullying—it doesn't matter who the child is who is being victimized or what their academic station is; bullying by another child can result in serious consequences, which may or may not be readily apparent for the bullied child.

In the case of the gifted child, the parents need to pay special attention to them without making the child feel singled out or "different"—it is a delicate balancing act, and one in which the gifted child needs the reassurance in spite of having special gift. Become their rock and guardian angel!

As we sought to have Brad enter the gifted program at this very early age, we discovered that camaraderie would be established with classmates who were similar in nature, including in terms of their academic abilities. This tends to discourage an atmosphere for bullying. The Exceptionally Gifted Program was designed for children with the expectation that they would remain with the same class from kindergarten through middle school and would be taught by educators who were very capable of understanding them.

Other characteristics of the gifted child includes their heightened sensitivity to their environment, as pointed out in a scenario the book *Giftedness*. Wayning offers a creative solution that can be adopted by any parent, whether their child is gifted or not.

The scenario goes something like this: Your child comes home one day complaining that "the work is too hard." You know from firsthand experience that your child does not have a learning disability, yet the complaint is there, and it is real. As it turns out, the work is effortless and not at all difficult; however, it is agonizing for the child to complete the work because it does not offer stimulation or is extremely boring. It is just the opposite of hard to your child—it is "easy."

One parent's solution in this scenario was to convince the teacher that the child needed more stimulating and challenging work. Parents should dig deeper to find out why the work appears to be tough. In this instance, the *boring assignment* offered mundane and simple questions about the story. To counter this, the mother was able to offer proof of her child's aptitude by writing a long list of books her child had read over a period of time, including science encyclopedias used as references. She also brought in articles on gifted children, which supported their need for more stimulating and challenging work. While the articles addressed the needs of gifted children, this idea holds true for all children. Students who are not challenged academically get bored and distracted and may start to misbehave, or demonstrate other unproductive traits.

When meeting with school personnel, parents are encouraged to not use the term "gifted," unless of course the child is in a gifted program, and the parent should be well-prepared with all information pertinent to the meeting. Again, the parent should offer proof whenever possible.

The end result in this scenario was an experimental agreement where the teacher allowed the child to bring his science books to his first-grade class and appointed him the "science authority." The other classmates loved it because now they had a peer to assist in providing answers, should they have any science questions.

While those who are reading this may frown or disagree with the thought of this solution, feeling that the child was singled out and, therefore, made to feel special, I beg to differ. This small suggestion, which largely served all concerned, offered a creative solution. In my opinion, this was a brilliant idea. Think with me for a moment or two: everyone would like to think they are special, and if thinking outside the box works to make that happen, even if only for a few students at a time, then so be it. All of us may get *our* turn to be special at some point in our lives; the earlier the better.

If you discover your child is learning at a pace beyond that of his/hers peers, there is nothing wrong with scheduling a conference, asking relevant questions, and offering suggestions to the teacher and/or administration. This could manifest in a win-win for all parties concerned. Become your child's advocate!

For more information, contact the National Association for Gifted Children.

*   *   *

The week prior to the test date, I informed Brad that he was scheduled to take a test on the upcoming Saturday; however, it was not something I elaborated on. As with the ERB test, there was no studying or preparation involved. A test is like a game to a child of that age, a four-year-old. Brad looked at me as if to say, "It's okay with me." I was confident that he would do well.

8.

QUESTIONS, CURIOSITY, AND CONCERNS

We cannot solve our problems with the same thinking
we used when we created them.
—Albert Einstein

On the morning of the test, Brad was alert, very perky, and somewhat excited, mainly because he knew he was going to go sailing with his dad that weekend. Shortly after our divorce, Al had purchased a used wooden sailboat, which stayed parked in a slip on City Island. Now a lot of Brad, Parker, and Al's time together was spent on the boat—usually beginning on Fridays right through to Sunday evenings—on the alternate weekends when both Parker and Brad visited with Al.

We arrived at the test site on time. Shortly thereafter, Brad was led off by the test administrator—a psychologist. About thirty minutes later, the tester brought Brad back to me and his grandmother, who had accompanied us to the test site. She informed us that Brad had started off fairly well with the test, but then he had begun to lose concentration, or something of that nature. I was shocked when I saw them returning, to the point that I could barely gather my thoughts. When I questioned the tester, her response was rather harried and vague; she then beckoned to the next child to follow her in for testing.

In the weeks that followed, I received the test results by mail. I was not surprised when the letter read:

Dear Parent:

Your child Brad Young was tested for the Exceptionally Gifted Program by a Board of Education psychologist and unfortunately did not qualify for admissions to the program.

It is the district's policy that children are not retested unless it is recommended by the psychologist. Thank you for your interest in the program.

The tester's remarks played over and over in my mind, and I began to get a little angry. The word *retested* unlocked the door to the arsenal I needed. I have always been a fighter, and if I saw it necessary to challenge something as important as this, I did.

Later in the day, I called the district office to speak with the head administrator, Ms. Cameron. I explained that my son was escorted from the test area earlier than expected, and I recounted my brief conversation with the tester. I also informed her that Brad was a very bright child and, as I did not see the actual test, I couldn't quite get a handle on the problem. I asked if she would be kind enough to clarify the matter for me. Ms. Cameron's conversation with me was rather distant and preoc-cupied, but nevertheless polite. She indicated that she would speak to the psychologist and get back to me.

A few days passed without a word. I decided to leave work

early one afternoon to go to the district office, taking a chance on meeting with Ms. Cameron in person. Ms. Cameron was a tall, stately woman with short, reddish-blonde hair. Somewhere in her early to midforties, she walked with a slight limp. One leg appeared slightly longer than the other, which may have been due to a birth defect of some sort.

My eyes scanned the room, taking notice of a Cornell University diploma hanging on the wall and pictures of two tanned tourist kids in front of some Greek ruins. We greeted one another with a smile while I stated my reason for being there. She summoned for Brad's records, and we immediately got down to business reviewing his test results. Ms. Cameron agreed that there were quite a few areas that clearly showed Brad's capabilities. She also assured me that she would look further into the matter and would get back to me as soon as she could. Upon leaving, I was friendly but firm, letting her know that I expected her to do just that.

August rolled around. I called the district office several times and left messages. My phone calls went unanswered. In the meantime, a lot of controversy existed in our neighborhood regarding the overcrowding of P.S. 106 and the possibility of busing the children to P.S. 180 in Co-op City. With the expectation of this happening in September, many of the parents, myself included, were apprehensively preparing ourselves for the busing. Needless to say, the school board members got their way. The first day arrived, and off our children went to P.S. 180 in Co-op City.

There was a great deal of confusion at the school bus stop: children, parents, and cars everywhere. Like many of the other families, Brad and I had decided to drive to the school.

Al promised to meet us there—while Al and I were barely communicating now, we knew that together our presence was necessary for Brad's benefit.

Aesthetically, P.S. 180 was pleasing. Fairly new, it reminded me of the elementary school I had attended in the early sixties, after having moved from Harlem to the Bronx. The tiles, the location of the stairwells, the positioning of the principal's office, all reminded me of P.S. 100.

The children lined up against the wall as their parents stood by. The parents were given their children's classroom numbers along with their teachers' names. The teachers stood by their respective classroom doors waiting to gather their children, as the parents followed. Al and I positioned ourselves in Brad's new classroom.

As the children scrambled to sit while the parents stood, a soft but raspy voice came from the other side of the room. Ms. Pratt introduced herself. During the next twenty minutes or so, she explained her teaching methods, along with some of the developmental milestones we could expect from our children over the course of the year. After her talk, Al and I agreed as we parted that the class size of thirty-three children was too large for a kindergarten class, but we were somewhat pleased by Ms. Pratt's delivery to the parents.

9.

THE CALL!

Ask, and it will be given to you; search, and you will find;
knock, and the door will be opened for you.
—The Bible

Two days later, Ms. Cameron, the head administrator from the district office, called.

"Mrs. Young, I met with Barbara Cole, the psychologist who administered the test to Brad, and as you and I discovered, part A of the test definitely showed your son's capability to succeed in the Exceptionally Gifted Program. After much consideration, both Ms. Cole and I agreed that Brad would benefit as a student in the gifted class." She paused, then continued, "Is it possible for Brad to start class next Monday? I know the school term has already begun, but only by a few days."

Without hesitation, I accepted the offer. "Yes!" I replied.

"Okay, P.S. 83, as you may know, is located on Rhinelander Avenue. On Monday morning when Brad starts, please see Ms. Reno, the assistant principal."

"All right," I said excitedly. "I appreciate all of your help; thank you."

We said our goodbyes.

Later in the day, although I was ecstatic, I wondered if a spot would have become vacant had I not been so persistent and raised concerns about the test.

On Monday, Brad began his first day of class at P.S. 83 in the Exceptionally Gifted Program. Judging from appearances, it seemed as if the fifteen children were somewhat handpicked: among them, there were Sara, who was Asian; one Middle Eastern child, Rashad; one Latino, Alejandro; and one African American child, Brad. The program was set up so that all would remain together year after year until they reached the high school level.

The predominately white school, set in a predominately middle-class Italian neighborhood, was located in the Morris Park section of the Bronx. Because we lived a distance away, Brad was scheduled to take the school bus, which stopped across the street from our apartment building. Although this service was available, many days I chose to drive Brad to school on my way to work.

Having already attended preschool for two years, Brad adjusted to the structured environment quite well. His teacher, Clara Hull, was a gentle, spirited person who adored Brad for his intelligence. Enthusiastic in nature, Clara Hull had been a teacher in the public school system for many years, with the majority of those years spent teaching gifted children. Ms. Hull lived on the Lower East Side of Manhattan with her husband, who was a professional violinist. They had no children of their own. Clara Hull drove to work in the Bronx each day and appeared to enjoy her job tremendously.

The first and second years went fairly well for Brad, with only a few minor problems here and there.

*   *   *

As time passed, the gifted program began to lose funding. The class size grew from fifteen to twenty-six children. A twin brother and sister of Caribbean descent and another African American boy named Raymond joined the class, as well as a few other children. This brought the number of children of color up to seven, including Brad. Now that the class had almost doubled in size, it was becoming more difficult to find a place for them at P.S. 83 and plans began to form to move the program to a new school. Because of the prospective change, the parents of the gifted classes were urged to attend the regularly scheduled school district meetings. During one of the meetings, we learned that our children were expected to relocate to P.S. 153, a school where a spacing problem already existed. Many of the parents, including me, objected to the move. To make matters worse, there was talk of increasing the Exceptionally Gifted class size even further, from the existing twenty-six to thirty. We knew it was going to be difficult for children to learn in an environment that was literally bursting at the seams.

Over time, the controversy continued. The voices of the parents objecting to the move became louder and more persistent, which still resulted in no change.

The gifted fifth and sixth graders of P.S. 83 were to be moved the following fall. It was now October. Brad was one month into the fourth grade. My thoughts were racing as to what steps to take next. After all, I had slowly become disenchanted with P.S. 83 for several reasons. The year before, Brad had been labeled as "disruptive" by his third-grade teacher. Labeling, as we know, can bring about a host of major problems for a child in any school system—public, private, or otherwise. It's a determining, preconceived notion of how a child will behave, whether it is done verbally by teachers or the administration or noted in the child's school record. The first incident occurred during the third grade when the gifted class had been scheduled to take a three-day end-of-year trip. Both educational and pleasurable, the trip was to be chaperoned by the teacher and volunteer parents. Traditionally, it was a perk for the third-grade gifted class, and it was something the children looked forward to from the beginning of the school year.

About three weeks prior to the trip, Brad and Rashad were asked not to go on the trip because of their roughhousing in the classroom. It had been nothing serious at all, from what we could sense, just a little horseplay between the two friends. Both boys were upset by the decision. Rashad's mother, Bonnie, Brad's dad, and I requested a meeting with the principal and Ms. Walsh, the third-grade teacher. We felt the punishment was far too harsh and that the boys' behavior did not warrant having them excluded from a trip they had so much looked forward to. At the onset of the meeting, Bonnie, a recent divorcée with a doctorate in education and behavioral psychology, was armed to resolve the matter. Al and I were prepared as well.

As the meeting progressed, though, it began to get a little heated. At some point, we knew we had to lay down our armor.

The realization kicked in that their decision was firm and under no circumstances would it be changed. Brad and Rashad could not go on the trip.

As disappointing as that was, both boys managed to live through the decision, but the situation left a slightly bad taste in my mouth. What had been evident during the meeting was the lack of support from an administration that could clearly see we were very much interested in the emotional well-being of our children and wanted to spare them humiliation.

Brad and Rashad were sensitive, gentle spirited yet assertive bright boys who were now labeled. This incident seemed to have traveled school-wide. Comments from a few parents and school personnel let me know that the outcome of the meeting had not remained behind closed doors.

At the time, Brad and Rashad were the only two children in the class with recently divorced parents. Both fathers, however, remained involved in their sons' lives and were dedicated to their education. In my estimation, teachers who are made aware of these special circumstances should look to support the child more than usual. I did not sense any sensitivity from Ms. Walsh nor the principal, Ms. Reno. They were aware of the situations, but they made no allowances in their interaction with either of the boys. Beverly Walsh humiliated Brad several times when she emptied the contents of Brad's desk onto the floor while the other children looked on, as he was being tugged, prodded, and ordered to pick up his things and put them in the desk neatly. Additionally, I was informed during a parent-teacher conference that Brad had been asked on a few occasions to spend the day in another classroom as punishment. This meant that he missed daily assignments and that his work had to be made up. These situations were not pleasing to me as a parent.

We have since lost contact with Bonnie and Rashad. The last time we talked, Rashad was doing well and had remained in the Exceptionally Gifted Program.

10.

IDENTIFYING THE ACADEMICALLY ABLE

When something is important enough, you do it
even if the odds are not in your favor.
—Elon Musk

Despite the unpleasant episodes of the third grade, at the close of that year, Brad was honored with first place in the Citywide Interscholastic Math Competition. The event, sponsored by the *New York Daily News* and Kodak, was held at Lincoln Center. We were all very excited for Brad, his accomplishment, and the honor he was receiving. And now a school that had begun to somewhat alienate him suddenly embraced him for this achievement. His being honored was, of course, a feather in the entire school's cap.

In September 1992, Brad entered the fourth grade. His teacher, Mr. Mason, was a mild-tempered, petite man with salt-and-pepper hair who had taught gifted children most of his teaching career. He seemed proud of the fact that he was a veteran in the gifted-teaching arena. It was usually Mr. Mason's class that Brad had been sent to for punishment while in third grade. While Mr. Mason appeared to be a fair man and liked

Brad, I had my concerns that this could be a no-win situation. Given the growth of the class and my disenchantment with P.S. 83, I began my search for an alternative school and stumbled upon the Mott Hall School, located in Harlem and set on the campus of City College. The school was a small public school with a private school flair. Devoted primarily to students who were academically sound in both math and science, the school appeared academically promising. However, there was a lack of physical classroom space at that time, which was disturbing. The classrooms were so small and tight that a few of the classes had to be held in the administrative office. In addition, the principal could not assure me as to whether there would be a spot available for Brad in the upcoming fall. I would like to point out that today, the Mott Hall School has grown by leaps and bounds.

Again, a few years after my first time doing so, I decided to call the Parents League of New York to request an updated booklet listing of independent schools located in the region. I also asked for the telephone number to the Education Records Bureau Testing Center, since I had somehow misplaced my copy. I was provided the telephone number, and a listing of schools was sent to my home.

Diligently, I went over the list, ruling out those schools that did not seem suited for Brad as well as those that were geographically too difficult to get to. I had to stay focused on the fact that I now worked in Westchester in admissions for a local college, we lived in the Bronx, and most of the schools were in Manhattan.

Even the schools located in lower Manhattan, bordering Brooklyn, were too far to consider. Those located in mid- to upper-Manhattan were also a reach, but I kept my faith that all would work out by the beginning of the fall. The cost factor was also a huge consideration. That, too, would be on a hope and a prayer.

I called the Educational Records Bureau to find out when the next test would be given. The test was scheduled for that Monday, 9:00 a.m. The cost the first time around had been about $115. It was now about $215.

I kept Brad out of school on the day of the test. We traveled on an early morning subway during rush hour instead of driving, to avoid arriving late to the test site. Besides, driving and finding parking in Manhattan was always very challenging. A lot of the time, nearby garages were full, even as early as 8:30 a.m.

When we got to the testing site, Brad was promptly administered the test. He scored within the 95th percentile. In case this information is as confusing for the reader as it was for me, this means that on a national scale, only 5% of the children in the same school-age bracket scored within this range, which means that children who score within the 95th percentile are more advanced than 95% of the kids their age.

A few of the schools we decided to apply to were fully booked and did not anticipate an opening for the fifth grade. To begin with, I had chosen a difficult year to apply to independent schools, as one should consider applying to these schools at the kindergarten or first-grade level, depending on the school. This gives you a better chance of attaining a spot with a full range of choices. If you can avoid it, try not to repeat the mistake I made when Brad was entering kindergarten. Applying to only *one* school is not enough. Also, be aware that you must apply *one year* prior to the year you are planning for your child to enter.

There are several programs through which children of color can apply to enter independent schools: Most of the programs serve kindergarten, sixth, seventh, and ninth grade. One such program is Prep for Prep, which is a nonprofit educational program that identifies academically able, highly motivated children of color and seeks to place them in independent schools. The children who go through this program generally enter the independent *day* school at the seventh-grade level. Early Steps is another program by which children enter independent schools at the kindergarten or first-grade level. While both of these programs are regarded as highly successful, I decided not to go the Prep for Prep route for two reasons: First, the boys and girls had to be nominated by the principal—not a good relationship there—and second, the program involved fourteen months of rigorous academic work to be done after regular school hours. I felt that Brad could compete academically without the added pressure of attending school after hours. I will elaborate on both programs in a later chapter.

We were going to take a chance and apply at the fifth-grade level on our own. We set our sights on the Fieldston School, located in Riverdale; the Browning School, located in Manhattan; and the St. Bernard's School, an all-boy's school also located in Manhattan. After speaking with the admissions people at all three schools, I had developed a good rapport, particularly with the admissions person at St. Bernard's, Ms. Libby Foster. Libby has since retired, but I will never forget her for her overall interest in Brad and me.

Upon Libby's retirement from St. Bernard's in June 1994, Stuart Johnson, the *then* Head of School, wrote in one of the semi-annual publications, "As for Libby, for a generation she made sure that the right boys and the right families came to the right place—4 East 98th street, to be precise. The consummate ambassador for St. Bernard's, Libby radiated the qualities we wanted to see in the school and ourselves: high standards of style and character, warmth, respect for the work to be done, love of children, and great humor. Her smile captivated and she surpassed at putting nervous parents at ease on the tours of the school. In her easy way, she told them what they needed to know, showed them St. Bernard's at its best and, somehow made us comfortable, too, so that when the doors to the classroom opened, visitors could see—and stay and watch—real teaching and learning going on without self-conscience or the Potemkin-village quality one might expect. Her years of walking the school gave her unsurpassed insight into its strengths and weaknesses, and no one could be more tactful, yet telling in her, suggestion." He further wrote, "For all Libby's graceful, easygoing nature, she has a passionate conscience and deep commitment. She is the leader in St. Bernard's commitment to diversity, working tirelessly with boys of color and their families, both before and long after admissions. Her irresistible insistence that St. Bernard's be a hospital to everyone—and we all know how tough boys (teachers and parents, too) can be to one another—did much to make the school a civil friendly place."

The full essence of Stuart Johnson's comments about Libby Foster continued; however, as one can see, she was exceptional in her field. It was because of Libby's foresight and tenacity that room was made available for Brad in what we both knew was a difficult year for admissions. I will always remember her kindly.

In retrospect, all three schools, Browning, Fieldston, and St. Bernard's, liked Brad and the fact that he had scored in such a high percentile on the ERB test.

Although the schools took the time out for the admissions process, interviewing, etc., all were aware that they may not have openings. Nonetheless, they encouraged us to apply. As one admissions person pointed out, "Anything can happen." In other words, the odds were not in our favor; however, situations do occur when children may have to leave for whatever reason and a spot opens up. As a rule, the children generally began at the kindergarten or first-grade level and remained at their respective schools until high school graduation, depending on the school.

The first school to accept Brad was the Browning School, but they offered little in the way of a financial package. It would have been too much of a financial struggle for us to make up the difference in the tuition. As it turned out, a space did not become available at Fieldston, the school we were most interested in. Therefore, Brad was not offered a spot. Fieldston did, however, encourage us to reapply at the seventh- or ninth- grade levels, when a few of the children might decide to venture out or a parent's business might necessitate relocation of a family, leaving a seat available.

11.

GREAT NEWS!

Education is the most powerful weapon which
you can use to change the world.
—Nelson Mandela

In May 1993, the acceptance letter from St. Bernard's brought both tears and a sigh of relief. Not only was Brad accepted (thanks to Libby Foster), but the financial aid package was also quite manageable.

The acceptance letter read:

Dear Ms. Young,
It gives me great pleasure to offer Brad a place in our fifth grade for next year, and to say how delighted we would be to have him here at St. Bernard's.

[The rest of the letter went on to describe the financial package and additional literature we could expect to receive prior to the beginning of the school year.]

We look forward to hearing from you.

Yours Sincerely,
Stuart H. Johnson, Head of School

After receiving the letter, I called my mom to share the good news. My mother, who had been supportive but was also riddled with anxiety, joined me in my tears of celebration After we sobered up and ceased sobbing, Mom asked, "How's the financial part?"

"Oh, he'll receive a good deal of aid. I'm so happy, you would not believe," I said. "God is good!"

"Yes, he is," Mom responded. "Did you tell Brad yet?"

"No, he's in his room. I'll tell him when we hang up. I just called Al a few minutes ago, but he wasn't in. I'll call him later," I said.

"Okay."

"Okay, I'll call you tomorrow." We hung up, each basking in the great news.

Brad was finishing the year at P.S. 83 with the anticipation of starting a new school in the fall. Although St. Bernard's was located on 98th Street and we knew it to be somewhat of a challenge to get to each day, the effort would be well worth it.

In the summer following Brad's acceptance to St. Bernard's, the college in Westchester County where I was employed, experienced financial difficulties and had to downsize in a variety of departments. As one of the last hired, I was laid off. The news came as a blow to me that day, but I managed to recover and began to see my layoff as sort of a blessing. It meant I would receive unemployment benefits, which would allow me to gradually search for employment in Manhattan, putting me closer to St. Bernard's.

I had been accustomed to working in Manhattan and had worked there for many years prior to working in New Rochelle in Westchester. There was something about the energy of

Manhattan . . . the people, the fast pace. On the flip side of the coin, the thought of not having to work at all for a while appealed to me. I could spend more time with my son, driving Brad back and forth to school each day. The commute was about thirty-five minutes each way.

Financially, I had always managed to have decent savings, just in case there was an emergency of some kind. My savings combined with my unemployment checks made this perceived setback doable, at least for the time being. I later took on a part-time job at a newly established business school in the Bronx. I served as a career service coordinator/director. I was the department . . . no staff.

12.

NEW SCHOOL: REQUIREMENTS AND EXPECTATIONS

The will to win, the desire to succeed, the urge to reach

your full potential . . . these are the keys that will unlock

the door to personal excellence.

—Confucius

Brad began at St. Bernard's School in the fall of 1993. And, of course, we had some concerns about thrusting him into a white, upper crust, elite environment. While we had previously placed Brad in what one would deem a predominately all-white surrounding at P.S. 83, this was a completely different playing field. St. B's represented, as many of the independent schools do, an old English, old money (and in later years, "new money") Anglo Saxon environment. Moreover, unlike many of the parents whose kids attended St. B's, we did not come from money. Both Al and I came from working-class families that struggled to make a living.

Like St. Bernard's, the majority of independent schools were founded in the late 1800s or early 1900s. Most were, and are still, headed by an administrator called the head of school (formerly "headmaster"), a position similar to that of a principal in a public school. Stuart Johnson, Head of School of

St. Bernard's, was a well-read man, educated at Yale and quite
the example of gentlemanly refinement. As a daily ritual, every
morning, as the boys entered the door at St. Bernard's, Stuart
Johnson would shake their hands one by one. I suppose this
gesture was to remind them that they were little gentlemen, and
they should act and be treated as such.

After having read the first few pages of the St. Bernard's
detailed handbook, I felt that my belief that Brad would
do just fine there was somehow confirmed. In part, the
handbook read:

> St. Bernard's wishes to give motivated young boys of
> diverse backgrounds from the first through ninth grade
> an exceptionally thorough, rigorous, and enjoyable
> introduction to learning and community life. We wish
> chiefly to inspire boys to appreciate hard work and fair
> play, develop confidence in themselves and consider-
> ation for others, and to have fun doing these things.
> The following premises underlie our work and give the
> school something of its character:
>
> 1. It is important both to challenge boys and to
>   show great affection for them. Indeed, children
>   are bored if not challenged and dispirited if not
>   engaged by their work.
> 2. A regard for the beauty and power of English—in
>   reading, writing, speaking, listening—and mastery
>   of numbers are delightful in themselves and
>   indispensable for future success. Learning how to
>   learn is of first importance.

3. Close behind comes the need for a traditional body of knowledge that we consider basic. With a sound educational method and sufficient cultural background, our students can be in touch with their past and so confront the challenges of the future with greater understanding.

4. Boys and teachers are encouraged to be individuals—without self-indulgence, it is hoped. Cooperation and teamwork are essential, but they come more readily if one's own identity is strong and generally accepted by others.

5. Families are and must be the primary source of vital curiosity, habits of discipline, ethical values, and good manners, but given the difficulty of inculcating these virtues, they deserve all the help they can get from us.

6. A good heart is finally more valuable than a well-stocked, well-trained head.

St. Bernard's currently consists of grades kindergarten through nine (there was not a kindergarten during Brad's attendance), separated by three divisions: the junior school, grades kindergarten through three; the middle school, grades four through six; and the upper school, grades seven through nine. The overall population of the school was approximately 288–300 boys, with an average class size of twenty students or fewer—a perfect class size, in my estimation.

Brad was entering the middle school. By that time, the boys who had reached middle school age were expected to learn languages: French, then Latin. Note-taking was high on the agenda as well and was introduced in history and science classes. In addition, the students were provided a recommended reading list of both fiction and nonfiction books. The list was composed of books which had to be read prior to graduating from St. B's.

By the sixth grade, toward the close of the day, the boys were expected to attend a one-and-a-half-hour mandatory supervised study period. During that time, they started, if not completed, many of their homework assignments. Homework was assigned daily. If a child was out ill for a day or two or any extended period of time, the parents were expected to pick up the homework from the front desk at the end of each day. Missing assignments was not encouraged.

While St. Bernard's was academically rigorous, the school also believed that work should be balanced with play. Athletics were noticeably strong at St. B's, and all the boys were expected to take part in the athletic programs. As the school stressed, its goals were to develop a boy's skills, cultivate his sense of teamwork and sportsmanship, and help him to channel and release energy, all while having fun. St. B's was directly across from Central Park and therefore situated in a perfect location to play sports.

While they played against a few of the surrounding Manhattan independent schools in baseball, soccer, lacrosse, hockey, and basketball, many of their games were played away at Greenvale and other schools on Long Island.

On the days when "away games," as they were called, were played, the boys generally arrived back to school at about 6:30 or 7:00 p.m. On those days, I sympathized with Brad and his teammates, especially as they approached seventh and eighth grade, when their homework assignments were lengthy and more demanding. Brad usually started his homework in the back seat of our car on the way home.

St. Bernard's treated their boys with the best of everything, and coach buses were provided to bring them to and from the games. There were those evenings, while I sat in the car waiting for the bus to arrive, that I thought to myself how fortunate we were. Philosophically, I have always thought—well, I can't say *always*, but I'd say in the last twenty years or so—that you pretty much get from life what you expect. This was something I picked up from a woman I once worked with, one whom I both liked and respected. She was a bit older than me, divorced, and had raised two boys. Carol frequently had a story to tell about how lavishly she treated her sons when they were growing up. I didn't have any children at the time, and for the life of me, I couldn't understand her adoring treatment toward them. One day I made a comment that she may possibly be spoiling them. Carol let me know that that was not the case. She had insisted that all she wanted was to make certain that her boys experienced a good life, and not just materially. Carol wanted them to expect all the good things that life had to offer. She emphasized that people generally get what they expect. "If you expect nothing, you get nothing, and vice versa," that was Carol's mantra. What she said stayed with me over the years, so when I had Brad, I made certain that he was exposed to as much as possible from the beginning: traveling, dining out, concerts, children's plays, etc., whatever would expand his vision of the world and himself in it. Making plans for this became a priority.

At lunchtime, St. B's provided the boys with good nutritional meals that included a salad bar with everything imaginable.

More impressively, homemade pies usually garnished each dining table during the holiday season. In hindsight, the parents were not treated too badly either. We were indulged with gourmet appetizers and cocktails during the frequent after-school performances and parents' meetings. As part of our parental commitment to the school, once per year all the parents, both fathers and mothers, were expected to sign up for Safety Patrol Walks. This was a very small request for the school to make, and the parents responded graciously. No matter how affluent they were or how demanding their work was, they honored their commitment.

At the beginning of each school year, the parents were provided a list of names, addresses, and phone numbers of each child and parent, as well as a yearly calendar of events. St. Bernard's was extremely diligent about communicating with parents. Duplicate literature was always sent to the parents who lived in separate households. Although Brad's former gifted program at P.S. 83 was rather good about communicating with parents, I have found that some inner-city public schools are generally not as communicative. The parent usually receives the bare minimum amount of written literature from their child's school. During the, time Brad was growing up, the most a parent could expect from the inner-city public schools was a permission slip for a trip or a note informing the parent of teacher-parent conference night. What a disgrace! Communication between the parents and the school is critically important. I know that often lack of communication has to do with budgetary issues, which in itself is a whole other subject, but frequent written communication between school and parent should be a priority. And to think, I have enough correspondence collected over the years from St. B's to start a small bonfire!

For those parents who are interested in further reading about school budgets and the extremes of wealth and poverty in the American school system, I have discovered quite a resource. An invitation is extended for you to read *Savage Inequalities,* a book written by Jonathan Kozol. This Harvard graduate and former teacher has written a half dozen books on this subject, shining a spotlight on the funding disparities between inner-city schools and the public school districts that serve the wealthy. Kozol provides extensive insight from a hands-on study comparing public schools and the disparity of dollars spent per child in each school. Although *Savage Inequalities* was written more than a decade ago, sadly, the same disparities still exist today. In my opinion, it is one of the best books written on this subject; it is a good read, although a bit disturbing. Just be prepared for the wide range of emotions you may experience and endure while reading it.

*   *   *

On a different note, but categorically the same, as early as the 1800s, our ancestors have given rise to many profession such as doctors, scholars, lawyers, educators, and nurses through education. They have in turn paved the way for us to recognize the value of this responsibility, act on it, and pay it forward.

The book *Hidden Figures* by Margot Lee Shetterly, offers a perfectly vivid example worthy of the attention and careful evaluation of the adults and the youth of our day. For these professionals to arrive at their goals, many had to endure obstacles that are too painful to even imagine. For example, the women of *Hidden Figures* who worked at the National Aeronautics and Space Administration (NASA) were exceptional scientists, including mathematicians and physicists, yet for more than a half century, they were not acknowledged publicly—not so much as a whisper—for their stellar work in the space program.

Other examples include trained surgeons of color who were not allowed to practice in leading white hospitals, lawyers who were banned from practicing law in prestigious law firms, and well-trained bankers who were unable to display their talents in the financial world. They instead were pushed out of their industries or forced to accept lower paying positions within their industries. These trailblazers had to sacrifice their dignity, as they were forced to swallow their pride, all the while continuing to make inroads in education for their generations and generations to come.

As adults, we have a responsibility to those who came before us to forge ahead and secure an education, that offers cultivation of skills, abilities, and an outlet for their unique creativity across the disciplines that is uniquely ours.

Access to a comprehensive education holds the key to unleashing opportunities that can benefit all of humanity. We need not apologize for seeking a "respectable" education, something we are all clearly eligible to receive. It's how we go about making this happen that will be the deciding factor.

13.

EXPOSURE, PREPARATION, AND COMPETITION

Your success is not final – nor is your failure
—George Matthew Adams

At the onset of the school year, the parent volunteers stuffed and sent out mailings regularly. The Parents Association requested parent volunteers for a number of activities, including preparation of author and guest speaker' nights, community service, library events, the new boys committee, Parents in Action, and archives. I usually volunteered for the book fair and the new boys committee, assisting with incoming minority students.

St. Bernard's hosted a myriad of social activities to satisfy both the boys and the parents. Some of these activities included an annual ice-skating event called "The Great Skate" held at Wollman Rink in Central Park, Grandparents Day, Sports Day, prominent guest speaker events, and Author's Night, which featured guest novelists such as Jamaica Kincaid and Richard Ford. Also hosted was an annual fathers' dinner, a spring concert, a book fair, an evening Shakespearean play performed by the eighth graders, a spring jamboree held at the Puck

Building in Lower Manhattan, and a drug awareness program. For parents, there were several cocktail receptions. The "*St. Bernard's School Christmas Carol*" was held at the Madison Avenue Presbyterian Church, and there were numerous parents' visiting days. This was surely enough activity to keep one busy! Additionally, the school also hosted several black-tie fundraising events throughout the year, none of which I attended, largely due to the cost involved.

Funds raised from gift-giving are a large part of the school's endowment. These funds aid and support those students who are in need of financial assistance, like Brad. As the schools' graduates grew older and more financially established, they, too, as alumni, were expected to give annually to their alma maters. Annual gift-giving is usually encouraged by all independent schools. We always gave whatever we could afford each year.

As a parent of a St. B's boy, I was friendly and most often exchanged pleasantries with the other parents I met while I dropped off and picked up Brad from school or volunteered my services. As it was, however, many of the parents and I had little in common; our lifestyles were worlds apart, except for our shared commonality—our boys.

Most lived close to the school in doorman buildings. We lived in the Bronx in an apartment complex. Most were wealthy; we were not. The majority of the mothers were stay-at-home moms, while I worked outside of the home. Most of the households were two-parent households; ours was not. Although the lifestyles were different and we were not as materially endowed as other St. B's families, we were content with what we had as middle-income people; I felt blessed with our strong family ties.

In an effort to diversify Brad's daily activities separate and apart from St. Bernard, I enrolled him in the Harlem Little League to play baseball on Saturday mornings. My brother was a volunteer coach for the Little League organization. The league's sponsor was New York Congressman Charles B. Rangel, who later became the first African American to chair the Ways and Means Committee. My brother convinced me to have Brad join the league to train and play during baseball season. Here, he would have the opportunity to interact with more children of color and to build relationships.

Brad didn't mind the drive into Harlem on Saturdays. I hesitated at first, giving up part of my weekend when chores were to be done, and besides, having to travel to collect Brad on some late evenings during the week, when he had soccer and lacrosse away games. To my surprise, the sacrifice turned out to be an outing I began to look forward to. The weather on those Saturdays was almost always beautiful . . . and breathtaking, as spring slowly made its approach. Early morning traffic on the drive to the baseball park was minimal or relatively nonexistent, as was traffic on our ride home. Before heading home to the Bronx, we always stopped at the nearby (the well known) Sylvia's Restaurant for a late breakfast or brunch. That always brought the afternoon to a pleasant close.

Brad was involved in baseball for about three years before he said he would rather focus on soccer, which was also hosted by the Harlem league.

*　　*　　*

By the time Brad's second year at St. Bernard's rolled around, I had befriended several mothers of color. Grace lived in Co-op City in the Bronx, not far from where we lived. Lillian lived in Brooklyn, and Sara lived in a brownstone in Harlem. Grace, a divorced single mother who lived with her son, Liam, had been a public school teacher in the Bronx for many years, and she later served as a member of the board of directors at St. Bernard's. Lillian, mother of Cooper, was a widow of a few years and a professor at one of the local universities. Sara, whom I have remained in close contact with, was employed in finance and lived in Harlem with her son, Alfonzo, her husband, and her daughter. Independent private schools were not new to Sara; she had gone through this process with her daughter some years before.

Unlike Lillian and me, Sara and Grace had sought the independent schools through the Early Steps program, which, as I mentioned earlier, assists parents and children in the selection of appropriate independent schools at the kindergarten and first-grade level. In hindsight, had I known about the Early Steps program when we were applying to kindergarten, we certainly would have used this service, which may have prevented the disappointment we experienced the first time we applied to the independent schools. Because all of us were mothers of children of color, our friendship was one of support to one another, and we communicated as often as necessary about our sons and the school.

My friend Alice, whom I had befriended many years before, was the person I spoke with almost daily and with whom I shared my deepest thoughts and concerns regarding Brad's schooling. Alice was what I considered a veteran at the independent school business. She and I would discuss any problems Brad, or her son, Santiago, (who attended a different independent school in Manhattan) may have encountered during the school year, and together we'd figure out an appropriate course of action. There were times when I questioned why we had placed our children in an Anglo, upper crust environment, and Alice would always remind me that in the *real* world—the *work* world—both boys would have to be prepared to compete. This was the preparation part.

Sara and her son, Alfonzo, Brad, and I would vacation together, attend shows, and eat out occasionally. We wanted to ensure that the boys remained close. Alfonzo was a couple of grades behind Brad, but when you are that age, you really don't care. Liam and Cooper were in the same grade as Brad. As the boys began to get older and go their separate ways, the contact lessened, however. All attended separate high schools—three attended boarding high schools, while Liam attended Fieldston in Riverdale. As of this writing, all of the boys have attended leading Ivy League or other prominent colleges.

Working part-time, I continued to drive Brad to and from school. As time progressed, I acquired full-time status at my place of employment and, as a result, began to look for a way by which Brad could travel to and from school alone. The express bus line closest to our apartment stopped too far away from the school. Searching, I found another express bus line located near where I worked, and this one dropped Brad off a half block from his school. Therefore, when I began full time, I drove Brad to the bus stop each morning, a plan that worked out great. After a while, most of the express bus drivers knew us both by face, and I felt comfortable with the decision to let Brad travel by himself.

Every month, we purchased commuter tickets for the bus;

I found it to be well worth the money, and it gave Brad a sense of autonomy, which is something a child needs to feel at that age. After all, he was now finishing sixth grade. By the time the seventh grade rolled around, Brad was taking the public bus to and from the express bus line.

14.

SWIFT TRANSITIONS: A FELT NEED

It does not matter how slowly you go as long as you do not stop.
—Confucius

Time flew by so quickly. Before we knew it, we were considering the options for our next steps. Should Brad remain at St. B's for the ninth grade or apply to a boarding high school? St. Bernard's only went to the ninth grade, so, by the time eighth grade rolled around, the boys had to decide whether to continue there for one more year or move on to another day or boarding school. At the time, as I understood it, leaving St. B's in the eighth grade was the more popular decision. That is, getting into an independent high school of one's choice in the tenth grade becomes difficult because most of the spots are pretty much filled. Applying for the ninth grade is much less competitive.

Historically, three to fifteen boys remained at St. Bernard's out of a group of thirty. The decision seemed to depend upon the class. For example, in the class prior to Brad's graduating class, only three boys chose to remain, while eleven boys decided to remain in Brad's class. It was quite unpredictable as to how many would remain or leave in a given year. The choice between staying and leaving was not an easy one for a family to make. The struggle usually centered on whether to have your child apply to an independent high school in the New York City area (there is a limited number of independent high schools in New York City) or apply to an independent boarding high school outside of the city or state. This, of course, would mean that your child would live away from home.

This difficult decision is even harder for parents of color, who know that their child will be in the minority away from home. Some parents may have gone to great lengths to build and instill strong qualities of identity up to this point. Sending a child to boarding school is very different from having them attend an independent *day* school—if your child attends a day school, you know they are in the minority, yet you are there to comfort them or perhaps buffer any rocky times and reinforce their positive self-image, whatever their ethnicity. Sending them to boarding school is not the same. You are not there for them on a daily basis; it's an emotional struggle to let go.

Boarding schools were a new concept for me, even when Hannah announced she was going to attend a boarding school in Pennsylvania. While she was there, I learned a little bit more about some of the day-to-day living from the stories she would share with me when she came home to visit during breaks. I also picked up additional information from Brad when he went to visit Hannah, and later Parker, at the same school.

Boarding schools were not new to the Black elite, however, as Lawrence Otis Graham, author of *Our Kind of People*, points out. Beginning as early as the late 1800s and early 1900s, the idea of boarding schools grew out of the South's refusal to build local public schools for Black students, which meant that the children who had advanced beyond the eighth grade had to travel great distances to attend high school. The alternative for families included sending their children north to live with relatives in order to complete their high school education. From this point, many parents who could afford it found it more advantageous to seek Black-owned boarding schools for their children, schools such as the Palmer Memorial Institute, located in Sedalia, North Carolina. This school was considered one of the top boarding schools in that region and one of the most selective and elitist. Set on a forty-acre campus, the school was owned and run by headmistress Charlotte Hawkins Brown, and it was modeled after the Andover School and similar white boarding preparatory schools.

Over the years, other Black-owned boarding schools emerged but have since closed their doors. During the time of these schools' emergence, only a few affluent Blacks sent their children to what were considered prestigious northern white boarding schools such as Phillips Exeter, Phillips Academy, and Northfield. Today, according to Graham, some Black families, elite or not, have embraced a boarding school education and don't even consider public or private independent day schools beyond the junior high school level.

At an earlier time, my mom belonged to a political club headquartered in Harlem, on the corner of 125th street around Lenox Avenue. Posters of political candidates lay on a back wall of the club. Because of my mother's affiliations, she had to attend political events quite frequently. I remember being a preteen and accompanying her at least twice each year to dinner dances honoring several civic leaders. On those occasions I dressed up in my crinoline-lined dress and black patent leather shoes and, in my mind, I was the belle of the ball. Today, I still have several of the journals where political figures, businesses, and individuals purchased ads; they, too, are among my keepsakes. Thinking back, because of my mother's political and thus social connections, we were once invited to a debutante ball; that is, where the Jack and Jill children (as they are referred to) of the elite Black families are introduced to society. The parents sponsored and invited guests to these black-tie events to celebrate the rite of passage for a select group of adolescents. Back then, the event focused more on developing and exercising the proper social graces, but as time changed, the focus changed to education, forming networks, and fundraising to give back to the underserved communities.

While my young eyes were too naive to capture what the rituals were all about at that time, I remember those young people who were slightly older than I, the young women dressed in conservative, below-the-knee sequined dresses with white elbow-length gloves, the young men dressed in tuxedos.

Much later in life, I befriended Katlin Silvers, who at that time was the president of the Links, a prestigious women's group of the socially upward elite. In general, the Links are the mothers of the Jack and Jill children. Katlin and I worked in the same building but in separate businesses, and we frequently had lunch together. She was a humble-spirited person who had a house on Martha's Vineyard that she rarely spoke of, and she was one of the nicest people I know. There was nothing pretentious about her and nothing about her gave inference to the fact that she was of the Black elite. We have remained friends over the years and, when I am in NYC, I occasionally call her just to keep in touch.

In my estimation, many of the Black elite are to be commended. These families had to overcome discrimination that has plagued our race for generations. In essence, the Black elite who have "made it" are those we need to fully acknowledge. While my family is not of that distinction or spirit in terms of material resources or some exposures, we need to recognize those who, in past generations, have paved the way for many.

My life was different; my maternal grandfather, a quiet man, a farmer from Georgia, well-respected among his peers and those white southerners who knew of him, was a man of humble means. He provided for his family by working the farm while Grandma worked outside of the home. As parents, they made certain their children were high school educated and able to move past poverty. Granddaddy's family was only two generations removed from slavery.

Most of his children moved north for a better life, including my mother. And while we were not of the Black elite, I don't ever remember wanting for anything as a child. After my mom moved to New York, her younger sister came to live with us in Harlem soon after my dad passed, which was prior to my third birthday. My aunt, who was also my godmother, was single, worked a decent-paying job, and owned a fancy white Ford convertible to carry us around in. She bought my brother and I whatever Mom couldn't afford—but, of course, within limits. Our family's income came from the monthly widow's pension Mom received due to my dad's service in the navy.

Growing up, we were never made aware of any disparity between those who had and those who did not. Mom made sure of that. We always had good food on the table. I remember eating a lot of steak; I couldn't tell if it was filet mignon, ribeye, chuck, or what, but it always tasted good. Whatever the cut, beef had to have been inexpensive back then. We also ate chicken and fish; dinner was always a well-rounded meal that included dessert at every serving. In addition, we were always clothed well and appeared to have money at our disposal. If my brother or I needed school supplies or a new outfit, we were rarely denied.

I remember my aunt taking me to Arnold Constable—a store that may have been a step above Macy's, but not quite Berg-dorf's—to purchase a lovely coat with a matching roll-mitten or hand warmer. I was so excited! My mom would only allow me to wear the outfit on special occasions when it was cold. As I got older, my aunt paid for my singing and tap-dancing lessons. Every Tuesday, we would schlepp downtown to a studio near the Ed Sullivan Theater. On our way there, we often stopped at a well-populated music store in the 50s to purchase both sheet music for me and red-shelled pistachio nuts, which were the bribe to motivate my brother and me to go every week.

After a while, I couldn't wait for the recitals to come. One was at Carnegie Hall and the other at the Brooklyn Academy of Music. Traveling on the A train every Tuesday evening was getting to me. My brother professed later in life that he went along with Mom and me to protect us. I laughed. He was only a year older than me, and I knew Mom would never leave him home alone while we traveled into mid-Manhattan, so he really had no other choice but to come. When I think back, it was quite an experience for us as children to have witnessed the hustle and bustle of the mix of all New Yorkers, most of them leaving work at that time of day.

I loved my life as a child, though, of course, I missed my dad terribly. Aside from that, we had a strong family bond with aunts, uncles, and cousins on both sides of the family. My dad's parents were factory workers and lived nearby in El Barrio, Spanish Harlem, and we would often visit on Sundays, always surrounded by good Cuban food—black beans and rice and pernil roast pork—and lots of company. Hispanics loved to entertain lots of family and friends. It was like one big party every Sunday. Next-door neighbors would come in and out; no one locked their doors. My grandfather would always have baseball or old Cuban records by Celia Cruz or the like playing in the background. Our home on St. Nicholas Avenue was plenty lively, too, especially on holidays. Dad, who had worked in the Garment District, had been a struggling songwriter before he passed, so we had a piano in our railroad flat in Harlem. My aunt, who was the lively one, made sure we had plenty of entertainment. She loved her Sam Cooke and Chubby Checker records to dance to. On some Saturdays, after we left our Brownie and Cub Scout meetings, my brother and I would go the Apollo Theater, which was walking distance from our apartment. Auntie knew the managers and would arrange for us to go to the shows and go backstage. My brother and I loved it. Seeing Stevie Wonder, the Temptations, Smokey Robinson, and a host of other Motown talent was amazing and unforgettable! Looking back, I have come to appreciate the value of the exposure.

In addition, during most summers, we would go to Georgia to be with our maternal grandparents on their farm. Grilling my grandfather about his livestock and the smokehouse (where meat was cured) and picking blackberries for Grandma to make her delicious pies absorbed a great deal of our time. What a life!

Given our strong family ties, we didn't question the "haves and have-nots." The elite . . . who? The Jack and Jill . . . who? As I mentioned earlier, I appreciate those elites who were able to overcome the harsh—and many times ruthless—discrimination that we as people of color had to endure. "They" in many ways opened and paved the way for those of "us" who were of more humble means.

At St. Bernard's, there were two families of color who were of the Black elite. At that time, and as a young mother, I did not recognize the differences; sometimes I think I had blinders on. Although they never spoke of their backgrounds or the sort, they were very pleasant people. Both mothers and fathers and I would occasionally meet while picking up our sons from school. Both couples already knew which boarding high schools their boys would attend. The selected schools had been their own alma maters. In retrospect, I think about the demeanor of those two boys, their confidence, and how they mingled quite well among their white peers. Although they were rather different from some of the other students, I admired the comfort level they exhibited.

*   *   *

Decisions, decisions . . . the decision to attend boarding school was a tough one to make. And in hindsight, as we weighed our options, I wish we'd taken the chance and waited to have

Brad attend boarding high school in the tenth grade instead of the ninth. As he entered and sought to navigate this new stage of maturity, he probably would have benefited significantly from daily encouragement and direct reassurance, had he stayed home an additional year. Although we knew that St. B's was academically advanced, we hadn't realized that its reputation among the varying boarding high schools was so positive; Brad more than likely would have gotten into any boarding high school of his choosing, regardless of the grade level.

15.

3D: DETAILS, DIRECTIONS, DEADLINES (THE RACE CONTINUES)

Challenges are what make life interesting and overcoming them is what makes life meaningful.

—Joshua J. Marine

Rob Taylor, the placement advisor at St. Bernard's, worked diligently with all ninth-graders' families as we prepared for high school applications. A detailed instruction letter on how to fill out the application forms and a preparation booklet outlining the entire process were sent out well in advance to ensure the students' timeliness in meeting their desired schools' application deadlines. All materials were to be handled and processed through the St. Bernard's advisor's office.

In addition, each family was responsible for arranging a meeting with the placement advisor to discuss their son's interests, thoughts, strengths, and concerns. We were also encouraged to draft an essay about our sons prior to the meeting. This information assisted Rob with preparing his individual letters of recommendation on behalf of the boys, which were later sent to the schools. I wrote in a two-page typed essay, *"Brad is a thirteen-year-old boy who is good spirited. He possesses both intelligence and common sense and exhibits a spontaneous sense of humor. He is sensitive to the plight of others . . ."* and I continued to outline Brad's accomplishments and unique characteristics.

The application process was going to be long and tedious, requiring months of preparation. As Mr. Taylor pointed out in a letter to the parents, The next few months are important ones, and we should do everything possible to make certain that your son's academics are given the highest priority. Several guidelines were included in the application process booklet. For example, an *at-a-glance* information list on "Boarding Schools vs. Day Schools" read:

BOARDING SCHOOLS

1. He will live on a safe, spacious rural campus.
2. He will be living among boys and usually girls, closely supervised by people who are experienced in dealing within his age group.
3. The pace of the school is more relaxed. If he needs some extra help in math, he can meet with his math teacher after dinner.
4. He is likely to build close relationships with faculty who teach him in the classroom, coach him on the field and supervise him in the dorm.

DAY SCHOOLS

1. You want the responsibility and the joy of shepherding your son through adolescence.

2. He is a city kid. He loves living in New York.
   There are so many cultural opportunities here,
   which he is unlikely to find elsewhere.
3. Some students like to separate where they study
   from where they live. They like separate sets of
   friendships.
4. Boarding schools can be strict, high-pressured,
   competitive institutions. By staying at home, a
   student is able to enjoy a complete change in
   atmosphere each day.

Also included in the booklet was the calendar explaining
what was due and when, a matriculation list, school visits, a
rundown of what to expect, an overview of factors schools
consider when making a decision, guidelines for school interviews, questions parents and students should ask during interviews, and much more. The booklet also included an excerpt
from the book titled *Ask Your Mother: Family Life and Other Impossible
Situations* by Thomas R. Trowbridge III. I found a photocopied
section from the book, titled "Higher (and Farther) Learning,"
to be very funny and entertaining. You're sure to get a laugh
from it.- I recommend finding a copy.

After careful consideration, we chose to apply to boarding
high schools. This time, I remembered from experience that
one should consider applying to *several* schools. There are no
guarantees your son or daughter will get into the school of their
choice, so *always* have back-up schools.

During the early part of the year, we received numerous
invitations from a variety of schools to meet with their heads of
school and admissions personnel. These preliminary meetings

would take place prior to visiting the actual schools, and all were located in Manhattan, in the homes of alumni, bene- factors, friends of the school, or parents of children who were currently attending or had attended the schools. We decided not to attend any of these meetings, but instead, wait and visit the schools Brad had considered applying to.

The journey to locate an appropriate boarding high school began in March 1996. Rob Taylor recommended schools, and we selected those that would fit our needs and Brad's aspirations.

George School, located in Newtown, Pennsylvania, was among the list of schools to visit. This school was one we were already familiar with because both Hannah and Parker had attended and were graduates of the school. Over the years, Brad had accompanied his dad numerous times to George School to visit with Hannah and Parker during their respective years there. Hannah, who was the older of the two, was the first to attend. The admissions director of George School, whom I later met, knew Brad quite well, and, as the time grew nearer to consider high schools, there was the expectation that Brad, too, would attend George School. As a rule, schools looked favorably toward a candidate whose siblings were alumni, and preference for financial assistance is usually given.

The Taft School, located in Connecticut, was one of the first schools we visited. While there were numerous schools located in the New England area, including Groton, Choate, St. Paul's, Exeter, Hotchkiss, and St. Mark's, we decided not to put too much emphasis on visiting these schools because it would have been a waste of time, as we were positive Brad would attend George School if accepted.

The majority of Brad's classmates had planned to apply to the New England schools, and because our son had been with the same boys year after year, I wanted him to experience a change of environment, both socially and academically. George School was a Quaker-based school, which meant that in addition to the social and academic change, there would also be a spiritual foundation that was not present at St. Bernard's. And, after sending away for their catalog and reading the first few pages, my feelings were confirmed: this was the school for Brad.

On the second page of the catalog, it read *Today the school community includes a diverse group of adults and students who value academic rigor and Quakers' commitment to service, social justice, simplicity, and quiet meetings of worship. The school's motto, "Mind the Light," reflects Quakers' strong belief in the presence and power of the Inner Light—that of God within each individual. The light makes each soul sacred and worthy of respect. In a Quaker school, teachers work to assure students of their individual worth, helping them refine their gifts that are already evident or uncover gifts that haven't been developed. They believe that if young people are convinced of their own values they will, in turn, seek and speak to the good in others.*

In addition to George School's philosophy, the school did not give lip service to its "diversity." This was evident from the catalog and our eventual visit to the school. Surely, this was a comforting factor.

The visit to the Taft School was somewhat of a blur. My immediate impression of the school was that it was very conservative, with some familiar characteristics that reminded me of a few of the other schools we had visited early on, back when we were applying to the Bank Street School. The environment was very formal, and there was no shortage of well-dressed, perfectly clothed individuals, both staff and visitors. I felt slightly intimidated, to say the least.

The visit was short. We thanked the admissions person for their time and the tour and left. Brad was enthusiastic; I was not. Keep in mind that this was his first visit.

Some weeks later, Brad, Al, and I drove to Middlesex School, located in Massachusetts. This was one of the high schools recommended by Mr. Taylor and if my memory serves me correctly, this was his alma mater. The Middlesex School was relatively appealing. The admissions person was warm and friendly, though the tour was rather lengthy. The environment, however, seemed less controlled than I would have expected in a boarding school. Both Al and I came to this same conclusion.

"Did you notice the kids in the lounge who were horsing around?" I said.

"Yeah, you're talking about the girl pulling on one of the guys?" Al replied.

"Yeah, then she threw the pool stick and almost hit him. And the lounge area seemed sort of desolate and out of the way. Are there no adults around?"

Brad interjected, "Mom, didn't you notice there was more than one lounge area?"

"Yes, I did, but you would think more adults would be walking around," I replied.

Brad, of course, welcomed the thought of what appeared as a loose and less controlled environment. What kid wouldn't? He had set his sights on applying to Middlesex. We went along with it, knowing that, if he were accepted, we would more than likely decline. At this stage, however, we were at least willing to give Brad some latitude in his application decisions.

Brad and I visited both George School and St. Andrew's School without Al. Certain that George School was the school of choice, we were less enthusiastic when it came time to go to Delaware to visit St. Andrew's School. One reason for our lack of enthusiasm was that, when we had looked over the school's catalog, I didn't remember seeing one student of color. To the school's credit, however, I did see two faculty members of color. Today, the student population is much more diverse.

Jim Caine, the admissions director of St. Andrew's School, was extremely receptive and friendly. Jim and his wife, a faculty member, were both from New York. The immediate connection made it easy for me to ask a ton of questions that would help us make a decision.

When we first met Jim, a smartly dressed, slender man with a spray of gray hair covering both his temples, he was smiling, his hand outreached as he moved toward us. He was dressed in a muted blue knit argyle-patterned vest, a collared dress shirt and tie, and khaki-colored pants—the typical academia attire.

Brad had asked a couple of days before we headed to St. Andrew's if he needed to prepare for the meeting. I could not think of anything, except to reiterate that the meeting was going to be like the ones at other schools we had visited. Nothing to rehearse. On second thought, though, a few minutes later, I said, "Why not point out one or two of your assignments or academic accomplishments that you are proud of? For example, having received the gold medal as well as summa cum laude praise on the National Latin Exam, with all fifty states and nine countries participating. Also, having received first-place honors in the City-Wide Interscholastic Math competition, sponsored by the *New York Daily News* and Kodak. These are the accomplishments, I think you should be proud of, and make known." I also reiterated to Brad that he should let his personality shine through. Adults loved talking with Brad. He could talk about a number of current events, and he was smart, enjoyed a language-rich environment, and read a lot—both books and magazines. I would say that for his age group, he was well-rounded and very articulate. I thought of him as *an old soul,* as some elders would say.

Once, during Brad's time at St. B's, I signed him up with one of the large casting agencies. There were no fees involved. The name of the agency evades me now—Bloom something or other. I cannot for the life of me find any literature in my archives on the particulars of this period! What made me consider pursuing this, I can't answer either—that one was just an interesting thought and I acted on it.

The agency had offices in both New York and Los Angeles. I'd asked a photographer friend of mine to take a few black-and-white photos of Brad. The photos were not grouped in a formal portfolio, but instead kept in an 8.5 × 11 manila envelope. Brad and I had discussed pursuing this endeavor, and he was enthusiastic about it. After all, he loved watching TV, even while doing his homework.

One sunny day, shortly after class, I asked Brad if he felt up to leaving the car parked by the school and taking the subway downtown to the agency. He agreed. The times were quite different than they are today; then, you could go to a business office and hope to be greeted by a receptionist, who might say, "Let me see if Mr. So-and-So is in and check to see if he will see you." Today, if you are fortunate enough to be greeted by a real person, you are in luck! And certainly, if you don't have a prior appointment, you have just wasted your time and made a trip in vain.

When one of the two women in the casting agency came out to greet us, I was asked to remain in the lobby while she escorted Brad back to her office. After talking with Brad for about a half an hour, both women approached me with Brad leading the way. They seemed thrilled by his assertiveness and talkative nature and assured me that they would be calling on him for either commercials or TV shows.

Brad was called to a few auditions for commercials, which he did not get, and one audition for the show *New York Under-cover*, which is no longer aired but ran for several seasons. It was an excellent show and appeared to be heavily viewed. We, as the general public, never know why some shows last while others don't. In any case, Brad was to play an eleven-year-old boy who had to shoot someone. They usually don't tell you the details of the character until you arrive at the audition. When Brad excitedly returned to the lobby, he gave a few details of what he had to say in character. I was seated next to some boys who were apparently seasoned in the business and had come for the same audition, dressed in designer jeans, jackets, and the like, most with cell phones in their hands. During that time, the early to mid-nineties, the average child did not own a cell phone. Heck, many adults, including myself, didn't own one. In fact, I remember starting to panic when the outside phone booths started to slowly diminish and eventually go away completely.

As it turned out, Brad did not get the part. No surprise, after he explained the character's role. There was nothing about Brad that was "street." He was a happy-go-lucky, nerdy kind of kid who had no acting training, so, without training, to jump into this kind of character would have been quite a stretch.

That was the last audition we went on. I had agreed to try it for a couple of months, at least until spring . . . and that was that!

*   *   *

A current junior and senior toured Brad and I separately while we visited St. Andrew's. The two students were neatly dressed and well-spoken. My tour guide had a British accent, which is sometimes hard for me to understand, but I did my best to calm down and center myself so that I would stay in the "now" and listen intently. Listening was not one of my strong points. My mind, for the most part, often had a way of wandering, usually in anticipation of what the person would say next. And many times, if there was an exchange of communication, I was focused on what I was going to say next or how was I going to respond. This is a poor trait to have and one that I consciously have to work on, even up until this day— stay in the present.

I was the first to return from the tour and rejoined Jim, the admissions director, in the office. Brad came in about twenty minutes later, chuckling with his guide as he entered the room. The visit was good. On the ride home, Brad willingly shared his touring experience with me and seemed enthusiastic about the overall visit. He appeared to be especially interested in playing soccer and lacrosse, games he was accustomed to playing at St. Bernard's. Brad liked the sprawling size and layout of the campus, which captured a view of the lake from many angles and locations. He was also enamored by the fact that he could ride his bike from one building to the next for his classes.

Dead Poets Society, starring Robin Williams, had been filmed on the campus of St. Andrew's. Much of the filming was captured in photographs that were displayed on the walls of one building we toured. Brad was curious to know if I had noticed the photographs and that the filming had taken place there. I assured him that I had seen the display and was impressed as well, though I think I was impressed for different reasons. It was good to know that St. Andrew's was on the map and not some unknown school in the backwoods of Delaware and that it had a stellar reputation. I had to chuckle to myself!

While Brad was too young to have watched the movie, which came out in 1989, when he was only six, he liked Robin Williams. Having watched him in *Mrs. Doubtfire*, a movie produced several years later, Brad, of course being much older by then, was able to comprehend and grasp the magnitude of this Golden Globe–winning movie. Robin Williams's character played a divorced father in this funny, yet very emotional, tearjerker of a movie. I believe Brad could relate to and identify with the character, being that he was a product of divorced parents. This is often a sensitive subject for any child in those circumstances.

The campus was serene and beginning to show signs of spring; it was simply beautiful! On the way home, we stopped to grab a bite to eat, and we rode the balance of the long drive in silence, as Brad was absorbed in reading his latest computer magazine.

Both of us were somewhat impressed with St. Andrew's; there was something about the school that was quite comforting.

Perhaps it could best be described as atmosphere. I could not put my finger on it; it was just a feeling and a mother's intuition.

*   *   *

Late October had rolled around, and the application process had begun. The time had now come to make a decision on which schools to apply to. A letter outlining instructions on filling out the applications was sent home to the parents. It read:

1. It cannot be emphasized enough how important these forms are. Neatness and thoughtfulness are paramount.
2. The sooner you hand these in to your teachers, the better. This is especially true for those applying to city schools.
3. Hand in as many forms at the same time as possible.
4. Fill in whatever information is required. Here are some of the most requested facts:
5. St. Bernard's (please include apostrophe) Address: *4 East 98th Street, New York, NY 10029*
6. Envelopes:
    a. They must be stamped. It is a good idea to double what you think it will cost. We do not weigh them.
    b. The return address should be *St. Bernard's School/New York, NY 10029.* <u>Do not use your address.</u>

7. All applications are to be placed inside the
   envelope provided. On the outside, write your
   name and names of the schools whose forms are
   included.
8. City schools do not always have forms.
   Nevertheless, you must include an addressed
   envelope.
9. Hand each teacher your forms and ask if he will
   fill them in. Do not leave them on his desk. This is
   rude and they may get lost.
10. Good luck.

The applications included recommendation forms to be
filled out by the teachers and the school advisor.

This monumental undertaking was now happening in full
force. And I really do mean *monumental*. Imagine the frustration
of working with someone who procrastinates . . . that was Brad,
writing and rewriting. Each application required a handwritten
essay along with answers to a series of questions. Here are a
couple of examples of essay topics:

Describe an experience you've had in which you weren't
certain of the right thing to do. How did you finally
decide what to do?

Which of the activities in which you participated has
had a major impact on your life and why?

As you can see, these essay questions require a great deal
of thought, not to mention neatness in penmanship. The

overall process was like pulling teeth with Brad, who appeared resistant. I am certain I aged ten years during this period, and my relationship with Brad became a bit more strained.

The Secondary School Admission Tests (SSATs) were given the last week in October. The cost was $48 then. They are about $145 now (not including late registration fees). These scores are particularly important and weigh heavily in the application. Brad did well on the SSAT. He scored within the 90th percentile in all subjects.

At that time, the fees to apply to each school ranged from $35 to $60, depending upon the school. They are about the same today. The fees are sent along with the applications. Keep in mind, however, that there are exceptions in which a school may waive the application fee, if requested. We did not seek a fee waiver. To tell you the truth, at this juncture, the level of frustration was so high that I just wanted to write a check, hurry up, and get the applications in the mail, instead of waiting on a decision to grant a fee waiver.

After the applications were sent, the independent high schools furnished the parents with a checklist citing the forms, recommendations, etc., that had arrived and ones that were missing from the applicant's folder for its completion. In addition to making sure all forms had been received, the parents were also responsible for submitting their financial information to each school.

A letter with detailed instructions was sent to the parents:

Dear Parents,
1. Please complete the Parent's Financial Statement (PFS). Make a copy for your records. Send the

original and appropriate fee to the School and
Student Service for Financial Aid in Princeton,
New Jersey.

2. Please send an official Photostat copy of your
    federal income tax returns, plus supporting
    materials, to the school's financial aid office.

3. If applicable, a form entitled "Parents Who Are
    Separated or Divorced or Have Never Been
    Married" must be completed by the noncustodial
    or natural parent. Send this form along with a
    copy of your federal tax returns.

For all parents who were seeking financial assistance,
filling out a *Parent's Financial Statement (PFS)*, provided by the
School and Student Service for Financial Aid, was required.
This organization, located in Princeton, New Jersey, provides
the financial aid analysis of families, which is then sent to the
respective private high schools, where the financial needs of the
applicant will be determined.

Filling out the forms for financial aid was not new to me.
Every year, I had filled one out for St. Bernard's, so that part was
not stressful at all. However, the usual coaxing and prodding Al
had to take place in order for him to submit the noncustodial
financial information in a timely manner. This always took a
toll on me.

16.

GRADUATION: A SURPRISE OFFER . . . WHY NOT ECUADOR?

*Let our advance worrying become advance
thinking and planning.*
—Winston Churchill

Prior to graduation, Mr. Jones, one of St. Bernard's teachers who annually chaperoned a group of eighth-grade boys on a trip to Ecuador, asked me if Brad could go with them this year. Having just made it out of the grueling world of application land, and not quite prepared to accept anything else that resembled change, my immediate and very real excuse was that we could not afford the trip. Mr. Jones, who obviously wanted Brad to join the group, indicated that St. Bernard's would pick up the expenses. He asked if Brad and I could join him and a couple of the other families for a film and discussion about the trip at his home on the following evening.

Brad, who had been standing nearby, overheard our conversation and begged me to go to the meeting. I said we would.

I tried my best to keep an open mind during the film and discussion, but the thought of Brad being so far away from home on a safari in Ecuador was out of the question. I am sure one might think that this was an opportunity that should not have been passed up, but I was not comfortable with it. Besides, Brad was leaving for boarding school at the end of the summer, which was enough letting go for me, and I looked forward to our family spending as much time together as possible.

Brad endured my decision and did not seem at all bothered by it. Relieved that his initial enthusiasm about the trip had worn off, I was more determined than ever to make this a good summer for him.

The following two weeks were spent preparing for the graduation . . . new shoes, blazer, a graduation gift, etc.

On June 3, 1997, St. B's held the graduation ceremony in their recently built gym, packed with siblings, grandparents, parents, faculty, and friends. The keynote speaker, William Banks, a parent and alumnus of St. Bernard's, captivated the audience with his winning speech. The applause mirrored that of the opening night of a Broadway play. Al, Hannah, Parker, and my mother attended the ceremony. Parker photographed the ceremony with his then-new digital camera.

Excited, Brad appeared both nervous and happy, flitting from one side of the gym to the other, congratulating and being congratulated by his classmates. Soon it would be time to leave to go to the after-ceremony celebration, which was held at Tavern on the Green, a rather expensive and renowned restaurant located in Central Park. Only parents and students had been invited, so we said our goodbyes and headed for the restaurant. Brad and I caught a cab over, and Al met us there.

Parker, who was driving, offered to drop my mom off at home. Parker was a good young man, quiet, reserved, and always cheerfully willing to help another person at any given time. He had recently graduated from a small, well-known college in Pennsylvania and was now working and sharing an apartment in mid-Manhattan with some friends from his boarding school. Hannah was living in Maryland and doing her residency in emergency medicine. She had graduated Yale a few years earlier with a degree in medicine. Hannah was now looking better than she had a year earlier. I had been concerned about her because she had been losing weight and was beginning to look drawn. She was a very smart young woman, yet the challenges of medical school were showing. At the graduation, she was her usual cheery self and had gained her weight back.

Weight had always been an issue with Hannah in her younger years. At about eleven or twelve, she was carrying baby fat and began to worry about her size. Hannah would marvel at my *then* slim figure as I wore my well-fitted jeans and she often talked about dieting. I would assure her that as she aged, she would lose the baby fat and welcome a lean body. Hannah was already tall. As I had predicted, she grew to be a beautiful, tall, slender-figured woman.

We would see both Hannah and Parker often, as they attended Brad's school events at St. Bernard's, birthday parties if they were in town, or just visits to the apartment. Al was very conscious of keeping the siblings close. Like most parents, he believed that siblings should build a solid relationship, so when the parents pass, they would at least have one another. I was always in agreement.

It was a gorgeous day. We gathered in the Tavern's sunlit room. The tables were neatly arranged and draped in very fine linen tablecloths. The table settings glistened in the sunlight. Al and I marveled at how good the food was as we talked, joked, and laughed with the other parents who sat at our table. I am certain all were relieved that the day was coming to a close and that our children had reached a significant milestone in their lives.

The boys had gathered at a few tables all to themselves to share their last time together. Restless as time passed, they began to move around rather wildly, tossing the cloth napkins back and forth, talking and laughing out loud. We knew it was time to leave.

17.

THE LETTER: THE EMOTIONS OF LETTING GO

Yesterday is not ours to recover, but tomorrow
is ours to win or lose.
—Lyndon B. Johnson

St. Andrew's letter from advisor Peter Wong:

Dear Sharon,

It is with mixture of sadness and joy that I sit down to write this final letter to you in my capacity as Brad's advisor. The reasons for this are, I hope, obvious. Brad and I have worked and lived together on this campus for four years, and any time one faces the end of such a rewarding relationship, twinges of melancholy are inevitable. However, those feelings are quickly overwhelmed with happiness when I reflect on how successful Brad's experience at St. Andrew's has been.

Academically, I think his spring term comments speak quite eloquently to both his strengths and weaknesses as a student. When he puts his mind to it, he clearly is capable of top-notch work in any discipline—the humanities as well as mathematics and science. His selection as this year's Scott Science Prize winner at the Commencement is further indication of his talent and potential. However, we have also seen this year that he is capable of dropping the ball at times, falling behind in his studies, and turning in work late. In choosing to matriculate at Princeton, he has selected one of the most academically challenging programs in the country, and I am certain that he knows that in order to thrive there, he must work diligently and consistently.

Athletically, Brad has been an active participant in a variety of sports during his St. Andrew's career. While injuries kept him from participating in team sports his last few terms, I suspect that he has found in weight-lifting a passion that he will continue to pursue in college and beyond. Although I regret his withdrawal from team sports—he was always cited by his coaches for his ability to help a team bond and flourish as a collective—I also am glad that he has found an athletic endeavor that he can pursue for many years to come.

In his time at St. Andrew's, Brad has transformed from a young boy to a young man. So that you can see what I mean, please allow me to share with you two stories, one from early in his III Form year, and one which occurred just several days before his graduation.

Reading over my notes on Brad in preparation for writing this letter, I was reminded that when he first arrived on campus, he had a great deal of difficulty settling down during evening study hall. To put it politely, he drove his corridor parents and seniors nuts with his antics, not doing his own work and disturbing others on corridor. After one conversation, I wrote the following in my journal.

"I have tried to impress upon Brad that academics are the most important thing here and that two sure ways to undermine his chances here are to do poorly in his classes and to disrupt the academic work of others. I hope he gets it. He needs to grow up very quickly, at least in this area."

Fast-forward to Tuesday night before the Commencement this year. I was on duty on Brad's corridor, and at one point, I was in his room, trying to encourage him and Owen and Daniel to continue their packing and cleaning. Brad suddenly stopped what he was doing and asked me if I wanted my graduation present now.

"Sure," I replied, expecting him to pull a wrapped package out from the depths of the clutter piled on his bed. Instead, he faced me.

"Do you realize how much people at this school love you?" he asked me. "Students fight to take your classes because they know you're one of the best teachers here, even though they know you're one of the hardest. I have so many friends who are jealous that I have you as an advisor because you listen to me and treat me like an adult. People here love you, and I want to make sure that you know that. It's sort of the thing you tend not to notice."

Brad was right; that is the sort of thing that I tend not to notice. And even if I had noticed it, it's important to hear that sort of thing every now and then. As I walked back home that evening, I was struck by how mature Brad had become, how perceptive, how thoughtful. Working with him these past four years has helped me realize how much time, energy, patience, and love it takes to do this job, and how wonderful the rewards can be.

And finally, I want to thank you for all that you have done. I can only imagine how much strength it takes to send a child away to boarding school. St. Andrew's is only as good as the people who form its community, and every step of the way, you have been a staunch supporter and advocate of the school, its faculty, and me in particular. With all my heart, I thank you for what you have given me and my colleagues the past four years.

With love,
Peter Wong

As you may remember from the beginning of the book, Brad attended St. Andrew's School in Delaware. He entered in the fall of 1997. The letter above had been written a couple of weeks after Brad's graduation from St. Andrew's. I was very moved by its contents and by the overwhelming thought of having to close one door and open another, neither of which came easy for me.

Peter, an exceptional individual with an unequivocal interest in all his students, both as an advisor and math chairperson, remained Brad's advisor throughout his four years at St. Andrew's. This mild-mannered young man, born on the West

Coast to Asian immigrant parents, had made Delaware his home. And although Peter Wong occasionally talked about life in California and his parents, he made no mention of returning to the West Coast when his sabbatical would surface in a few years. To date, Brad remains in touch with Peter.

The St. Andrew's environment mimicked home life for most of the faculty. Surely this was true for the head of school and his wife, who lived in a lovely house on the campus. In fact, many of the houses on campus were quite nice, each displaying their individual and unique structures. Most of the faculty and their families, including the many cats and dogs that wandered the campus, seemed very content and comfortable there. The picturesque and sprawling campus sat on approximately 2,700 acres of land and surrounded a pristine lake.

St. Andrew's was an Episcopal-based school that embraced and welcomed all students regardless of religious background and where students were encouraged to explore their spirituality while developing an appreciation for all religions and cultures. Members of the St. Andrew's community were committed to sharing equally in improving the world as engaged citizens, with emphasis on social justice and peace. Students were encouraged to actively involve themselves in community service and outreach.

Brad's entry to St. Andrew's was not seamless. It had taken a while before he adjusted to the new environment. Al and I had experienced some differences a couple of days before leaving for Brad's first day at St. Andrew's. In retrospect, it appeared that neither one of us was prepared to let go, and it showed up in the way we communicated with one another. I had assumed that Al would be a little more acclimated in "the department of letting go" than me, because of Hannah and Parker. But, as he later explained, "It doesn't matter how many times you let go, each time is just like the *first* time."

I had difficulty reading Brad, who, for a kid, had maintained a poker face throughout it all. I really couldn't tell if he was happy and accepting of the decision to go away to school or not. Beginning with the application process, followed by the school visits and the arrival of letters of acceptance, Brad appeared unmoved by it all. But, after all, going away to school had been his choice, a choice that had apparently been influenced by his trips over the years to George School to visit with Hannah and Parker.

18.

"MOM, DON'T WORRY, I'M OKAY."

It is during our darkest moments that we must focus to see the light.
—Aristotle Onassis

When we arrived at St. Andrew's on Brad's first day, he appeared somewhat aloof, and I could sense from his body language that he was a bit frightened. Nevertheless, had I approached him with what I sensed, naturally, he would have denied it. I had anticipated this reaction from the fact that I'd been asking him all summer how he felt about leaving and his response was always "I'm fine," and "Mom, don't worry, I'm okay." Each time he had a tinge of annoyance in his voice, as if to say, "Why do you keep asking me that? I can take care of myself."

As we walked along the school grounds, Hannah offered me some consolation for Brad's behavior by sharing about her first day at George School and how she had acted very similarly toward her mother . . . mostly by trying to avoid her throughout the day. This tough exterior was out of fear of getting emotionally bogged down and to protect both her feelings and her mother's when they had to say goodbye at the end of the day. Al reminded me that he did not go to school with Hannah on her first day, but he did go when Parker went away to school, five years later.

Although I suspected Brad's behavior and tough exterior were a cover-up for his feelings, I could not help but feel hurt and saddened. One, because he was not going back home with me, and two, because he was not sharing his feelings, which made the situation all the more difficult. Trying to put myself in Brad's shoes, I looked at it from a teenager's point of view, but I still concluded that I would have done the exact opposite—that is, I would have clung as close to my mother as I possibly could and let her know how much I would miss her.

I reflected for a moment on my own experiences, remembering the day I left for college for the first time and prepared to board the plane to travel 1,600 miles away to St. Thomas, Virgin Islands. I attended the University of the Virgin Islands my first couple of years before getting homesick and matriculating back to New York to attend Lehman College. At that moment of being dropped off at the airport, I'd wished that I could have changed my mind and driven right back home with my mother and brother. The fear of leaving was overwhelming! Keeping in mind I was a few years older than Brad at the time—I was going away to college, rather than high school—I remembered that I still felt ill at ease and somewhat fearful. Surely, Brad had to show *some* signs of discomfort.

I took deep breaths and bore in mind that I would see Brad in a month . . . and every month thereafter, including longer visits at holidays. That made it all the more bearable. I survived!

The day seemed to have gone by very quickly, and as it was nearing the time to leave, Brad disappeared with a few guys he had met during our last visit to the campus. As I remember, on that particular visit to St. Andrew's, which happened to have been our last visit there before the acceptance letters were sent out, the school had hosted a question-and-answer session. The session gave prospective students and their parents the opportunity to ask questions to a panel of current juniors and seniors. It had been a full day, and I found the visit to be very enlightening, as each student discussed his or her personal experiences at St. Andrew's. This very visit had convinced me that St. Andrew's was the environment for Brad, if he were going to attend any preparatory boarding school at all. I had decided during that visit that if Brad were accepted to both, St. Andrew's would surely be my choice over George School. I kept my opinion to myself, however, out of concern about influencing Brad's decision.

I thought back to the decision process. Sunday evening had arrived, the day we had set aside to make the decision. It rained all day that day. Brad and Al returned at about 5:00 p.m. from their last visit to George School. Out of consideration for the working parents, it was not unusual for schools to offer weekend visits; that schedule worked well for most working people. About an hour later, the three of us gathered in a nearby restaurant to discuss the pros and cons of each school and to see which of the two schools Brad had selected.

The decisions were due early the next week. All but the George School acceptance letter had arrived, but while on their visit there earlier that day, Al had been informed verbally that Brad had been accepted by the George School admissions person, and that a letter of acceptance would not be sent out until Monday.

Brad and Al had picked up something to eat on their way back, and I had already had supper. Al ordered coffee, hot chocolate, and pastries. My stomach was a bit too upset to drink coffee or eat a pastry, so I just sat nervously, waiting to see if Al would start the conversation I had secretly been dreading. I had been a nervous wreck all day and had pretty much picked at my supper.

Al and Brad filled me in on their visit to George School that day. Brad, who was sitting next to me in the booth, moved around nervously, playing with the individual packets of sugar on the table and sliding his elbows back and forth. He was practically cleaning the table with the sleeves of his blazer as he slid them back and forth. I'd asked him to stop.

Al leaned back in the booth and said, "Boy." He sometimes called Brad "boy"—I guess using that term stemmed from his southern upbringing. Al was from Virginia and was what I consider animated in character, and he always had something to say to make you laugh. Raised in a house with both parents and three siblings from his mother's previous marriage, he had attended undergraduate school in North Carolina, married, and moved to New York to attend graduate school at Columbia University.

Al and I met and married some years later after his divorce. Our marriage had not been an easy transition. Nine years Al's junior, I had little or no experience raising children; although Hannah and Parker seemed rather accepting of me, I couldn't help but feel that they wanted their parents to be together. Part of that was my own insecurity; however, later in life, I discovered while reading and talking with others that this is usually true and kids generally do want their parents to be together. Yet, if the incoming stepparent can accept the role of a loving friend, it makes life easier for all. In this way, they are not looked upon as trying to fill the shoes of the other parent.

"Boy, what school do you think you want to go to?" Al asked.

Brad, who had apparently forgotten that I'd asked him to stop sliding his elbows back and forth, stopped for a moment. With his elbows still resting on the table and his chin cupped in his hands, he glanced at me, smiling, and said, "George . . . no, no . . . St. Andrew's School." Now he was giggling as he looked back and forth at us.

All along, I had sensed that somehow Brad knew that St. Andrew's was my choice, so I waited, and then I asked him if he was sure. He said yes, this time with a serious smile.

The summer of 1997 was passing by rapidly, and although Brad hadn't gone to Ecuador with the group from St. Bernard's, we managed to travel to Tampa to visit with my grandmother. (My grandfather had passed by then.) Certainly, the visit to Florida didn't quite compare to a safari in Ecuador, but Brad liked Florida. Besides, he liked the idea of traveling just for the sake of traveling—boarding a plane, renting a car, and the whole range of activities seemed to satisfy him. Of course, visiting his great-grandmother was a treat, too.

When we arrived in Tampa, we spent some time visiting with relatives we had not met before, but most of the time was spent just relaxing, cooking, and eating. The day before we were scheduled to come home, we drove to Busch Gardens, an amusement park that Al and I had taken Brad to when he was three years old. Brad didn't remember any of it, but in my mind, it seemed as though it had been yesterday.

*　　*　　*

I hated to leave Tampa and leave my grandmother alone in her house, but we had to get back to what would eventually boil down to "a new way of living."

My Cuban grandmother stood 4'11" and was a pillar of strength. After Dad died at age twenty-five and rather tragically, she and Mom remained in close contact. She loved her daughter-in-law. Mom was easy to get along with; soft-spoken, yet she would speak her mind when she needed to. From what I was told, there was one thing my grandmother and my mom did not agree upon, and that was where Dad was to be buried. My dad was a navy veteran, so Mom wanted him to be buried in the military cemetery (where Mom is now buried, some fifty-plus years later) and my grandmother chose another cemetery in Brooklyn. Both were pretty much broken during the time of his death, so I think Mom just gave in to avoid causing more pain and to keep the peace.

My grandmother, "Granny," as all of her grandchildren called her, would swing between speaking English and Spanish, especially when she became excited or when speaking with my grandfather, who spoke very little English. When Granny referred to men who were not Cuban, she would always refer to them as "the American fellow."

I remember when I was about eleven, Mom developed the flu, then I got it. Since Mom couldn't take care of herself or me, Granny came over every day to take care of the both of us. I recall feeling so sick that the light, which was turned off most of the day, unless Granny came in the room to spoon-feed us, was blinding and hurt my eyes and my head. My entire body ached terribly. Since that time, I don't recall ever feeling like that again. I rarely if ever get a common cold, but I remember quite vividly that awful flu feeling and the dimly lit room. We were sick for at least a week or more. My brother stayed healthy, and Granny saw him off to school each morning. We finally recovered . . . and life went on.

My grandparents lived in New York for many years while we were growing up, before retiring and moving back to Tampa. Food was always the center of our Sunday visits when they lived in Spanish Harlem, including shopping for food.

Granny would drag us, either one of my cousins or my brother and me, to a place we called "under the bridge," formally named La Marqueta. These markets with the sawdust floors were under the Park Avenue Metro-North line in East Harlem, which stretched from 111th Street to 116th Street. As a kid, I was in awe of the wide variety of fish, including salted dried codfish to make bacalao cakes, and slabs of hanging meat. The markets, which were composed of several hundred vendors, also sold fruits, vegetables, grains, and spices. You name it, they had it! In the wintertime, it was cold. As I recall, there were no doors, just a heavy plastic that separated one market from another as we moved from one vendor to the next. Sometimes our visits to the markets were short, while at other times they were exceedingly long. If we were there too long for my liking, I dared not complain. Granny could sometimes be pretty stern. If we said something she didn't like, she would give us her stern look and snap; then the snap would trail off to a soft, loving voice to finish the sentence. It was as if she would catch herself to avoid hurting our feelings. But of course, she would never apologize. That generation was definitely not the apologetic group.

My Georgia grandmother was a bit more playful. We would laugh and tease with one another. She had a great sense of humor, and although she had a stroke while in her midfifties that left her lame on her left side, she was not bitter and moved around quite well. She could still cook, dress herself, make quilts, and walk up and down the stairs with her cane, and once she clobbered a small snake that had gotten in her house with it. We later found out that the snake was venomous when my uncle came down with his shotgun to kill it. Grandma had wounded the snake so badly with her cane that by the time my uncle got there, the snake was in no shape to move.

When we moved to the Bronx, Grandma would come and stay with us for months at a time. She also spent time with my aunt and uncle out in Queens. It was like she would run away from home, leaving my grandfather to take care of the farm and the house. Six or seven months later, my aunt and uncle would drive her back to Georgia, and so on it went, from Georgia, then back to New York. Both grandmothers knew one another and would always ask how the other one was doing.

Granny and Mom talked with one another almost daily. They always spoke in English. Unlike my dad, Mom was not bilingual, and she had sometimes resented it when Granny spoke to Dad in Spanish in her presence. She felt this isolated her. Dad had sided with Mom and asked Granny to speak to him in English when the three of them were together.

When dad was alive, he had wanted my brother, who was a year and a few months older than I, and eventually me, to learn the Spanish language. My mom had been outright opposed to it, fearing that learning a new language besides English would only confuse us. Go figure! But Mom didn't know any better back then. Now I somehow feel as though we lost out by not learning Spanish. Certainly, learning a second language at an early age has its benefits. To put it plainly, the brain is wired and has great capacity for learning languages in the very early years. For one to be able to juggle two or more languages shows vast concentration and improved memory and, in later years, may help to lower the risk of dementia and Alzheimer's.

Today, my brother, three cousins, and I, on the paternal side of the family, speak very little or no Spanish . . . not that I haven't tried to formally learn the language. My cousins may speak a little more than my brother and me because their mother, our aunt, although married to an American man from Pennsylvania, spoke Spanish outside of her household to vendors and the like. Therefore, her children were exposed to the language on a daily basis.

When Brad was selecting a language in middle school, I reenforced the idea that the Spanish language was very much a part of our culture; in addition to this fact, there were a considerable number of Hispanics living in New York City. Brad said he was considering French, and I asked, "Who are you going to converse with if you choose French?" He listened but did not take heed, and he enrolled in French the following year.

Brad took the class very seriously. As a matter of fact, he tested for Advanced Placement when given the opportunity while applying to high school. Today, he says he occasionally practices his French, but from what I can see, not with a real person.

*   *   *

When we returned to New York, I started to prepare for Brad's leaving for St. Andrew's; the balance of the summer pretty much focused on that. Over the course of the late spring and summer, we had received approximately ten to twelve letters from St. Andrew's, outlining needed information prior to Brad's start date. In one of the many letters I received there was a list of what students were and were not to bring to campus. I made sure Brad was involved; he had his list and I had mine.

Later, we received a notification that provided information on the opportunity for students to test out of a given class they were proficient in and to go into a more challenging Advanced Placement class. That was music to Brad's ears. He had been good in math and French and elected to take those two tests.

St. Andrew's provided parents with information to have someone other than the parent act as a proxy to administer the tests. We chose Tara, Brad's godmother. Tara loved children, was an advocate for education issues, had a master's degree from Howard University, and was a close family friend. A week or two later, Tara received a letter thanking her for agreeing to supervise both the Algebra 2 and the French tests, along with a package including the test, instructions, and a return envelope from St. Andrew's. The results were positive. Brad passed both tests and was placed in the advanced classes for the upcoming year.

Brad received a letter, copying the parent, from Peter Wong. He introduced himself and briefly outlined his role as faculty advisor. This also included his keeping tabs on how students were adjusting to school life, academics, athletics, other extracurricular activities, and dormitory life. The letter further explained that he would also act as a resource for parents and detailed what to expect upon their arrival to campus the first day. He included his office and home number, along with his email address.

The night had arrived before we were to leave for Delaware. Brad called my mother to say goodbye and promised to call her again in the morning. He and my mom were very close. Mom sometimes picked up Brad on the weekends, or she would spend the night over our house, just to be with us. In 1989, my mother lived with us in our apartment for a few months after she was robbed in the building where she lived and where my brother and I had grown up. The incident left my mother so shaken that she never returned to the apartment again, except to gather her belongings. After living with us for the few months, she moved into a temporary apartment and then to a senior apartment in lower Westchester. The apartment was not too far from where we lived in the Bronx, about a fifteen-minute drive.

As I was growing up, Mom always had a car. She used it to drive to and from her job as a paraprofessional with the New York City Board of Education. I remember when my mother passed away and I was going through her belongings. I gathered all of the many awards and citations she'd received. As she was modest in all she had done, I never knew how much my mother was appreciated by her employer.

My mother loved her job, but she grew tired of it over the years. The lack of discipline and number of unruly children, along with the bureaucracy in the public school education system, had slowly taken a toll on her.

Brad called his grandmother to reassure her that he would stay in close contact. "I promise, I'll call you, Grandma," Brad said. "You can come with Mom to visit as much as you want." His voice sounded strong and confident. "And remember, Grandma, I will be home once a month."

Although Mom had not verbalized it, I don't think she had completely grasped the idea of Brad going to boarding school. She neither condoned the decision nor condemned it. She just went along with it. I think, as parents and as we grow older, we learn to just support or give the impression that we support the decisions of our adult children. In this situation, I am almost certain that was the case.

During their goodbyes, Mom let Brad know how much she loved him and that she was there in case he needed to reach out to her.

"I love you," Mom said.

"I love you, Grandma."

Brad had finally gone off into a deep sleep. The house was quiet except for the television playing in the living room. Brad and I had been restless for more than one reason. Shortly before we headed to bed, after I checked my to-do list for the last time, a news flash had come onto the television informing the public that Diana, the Princess of Wales, had been in a terrible car crash and that she might not have survived. The news was a terrible shock, which added to my already antici- pated restless sleep. I called my mother to see if she had heard the news, and she felt as much discomfort about the news as I did. We talked at length about it before hanging up.

When the alarm went off, I longed for more sleep, wanting to sleep right through the day and into the next. I wished at that time that I could have pretended Brad was going to stay right there in New York City and that the news about Diana was not really true. I had followed Princess Diana's life for a while, and although our lives were miles apart, she was divorced like me, and one of her sons, Harry, was near Brad's age. My heart went out to her two boys. I could not help but feel saddened by the tragedy they were facing.

The next morning, Al came over with his SUV and packed all the things Brad was carrying with him, including a bike. Because of the size of the campus, the school recommended the students bring their bikes to get around on.

Having stayed up late preparing for the day and making certain nothing was left behind, I was unsurprisingly tired. I was emotionally drained and wanted this day I had been dreading to come to a close. Brad and I traveled over the George Washington Bridge, only to come to a complete halt. Traffic was backed up as far as I could see. I wondered for a brief moment if Al was stuck in traffic as well, since he had traveled a half an hour ahead of us.

Brad was mostly silent during the three-and-a-half-hour drive to Delaware, and I had the radio on low volume while it provided continuous updates on the sad news of Princess Diana. Otherwise, it was a gorgeous day; the trees had begun to have their green leaves replaced with some of the vibrant colors of fall. How welcoming! I tried my best to appear upbeat and keep what little conversation there was lively, knowing this was our last day together for a while.

19.

SEPARATION ANXIETY

The desire to reach the stars is ambitious. The desire
to reach hearts is wise and most possible.
—Maya Angelou

Leaving Brad was difficult. The drive back to New York was grim and tearful. All four of us—Hannah, Al, Parker, and I—had driven in separate vehicles to the campus. As I drove back alone, I wished I had asked my mother to come along for support. I had felt she wanted to go with us, but I hadn't asked her.

I stopped at a gas station to use the bathroom and to get a wad of toilet tissue to dry my eyes. I found little relief in listening to the radio. I flipped from station to station until I finally just turned it off. I did, however, find some consolation in the snacks I had purchased. Oreos and potato chips had become my friends those last few months. I had started eating them regularly and saw that I had gone up a dress size. I wasn't pleased with the change in my body, but what could I do? I was probably beginning to fall into a mild depression, like the feeling one gets when saying goodbye to your child going off to college but magnified tenfold because Brad was younger. As the months progressed, though, the feelings did get better, as I had anticipated.

*　　*　　*

A few days after Brad left, I received a letter from Tad Roach, the St. Andrew's *then* head of school, addressed to the parents of new students. The letter indicated that the first few days during the children's arrival had been good ones, and all were settling in. He went on to apologize to the parents for the lengthy wait during lunch and assured us of plans to improve the entire process. As a new head of school, but not new to the school, he welcomed suggestions regarding future *arrival days*.

St. Andrew's School, founded for the most part by the DuPont family, was created with a commitment to educate boys and girls regardless of their socioeconomic status. St. Andrew's had a fairly large endowment, which made it possible for them to provide financial aid to those who requested it. Even those whom I call the "partially wealthy" received the aid if they asked.

St. Andrew's was considered one of the best boarding schools in the United States and had committed to maintaining a roster of 265 to 270 students each year. Again, like many independent schools, small, intimate class sizes were the norm. This usually lends itself to better learning opportunities and outcomes.

Tuition the year Brad began was $21,000 per year. This amount included transportation for activities on and off campus (movies, malls, etc.), medication and medical supplies for on-campus medical treatment, and the shipping and handling of textbooks. The school also offered very comprehensive health coverage. If a family already had health coverage for their son or daughter, the school preferred that they use the school's. If the family insisted on keeping their health coverage, the school asked that the family provide them certain information to determine whether the coverage was as good as or more comprehensive than the school's plan. Many of the parents who received financial aid were only expected to pay a small fraction of the cost for St. Andrew's medical coverage.

The tuition was a lot of money to us, and it was certainly not affordable on our incomes. So, again, every year I diligently filled out the financial aid forms, as I always had while Brad was at St. Bernard's. Private, low-interest loans were available and designed specifically for an independent school education. Parents could borrow up to the total cost of the tuition.

Today, the overall cost to attend St. Andrew's is roughly $62,000 a year, and each year the cost may go up by about 5%.

20.

RULES, REGS, AND HONOR CODES . . .

The quality of a leader is reflected in the standards they set for themselves.
—Ray Kroc

St. Andrew's had a host of rules. A handbook was provided to parents regarding the policies and procedures of the school. We also received a campus directory, which included the office and home telephone numbers of the faculty and administration, as well as the parents (whether divorced or separated) of each student.

On the first page of the handbook, the head of school wrote a "Dear Parents" letter:

When I prepared to leave for college each term, my father and mother sat down and reviewed a few of their expectations with me. At the time, those meetings seemed unnecessary, but in retrospect, their advice, encouragement and wisdom helped me make good choices during those years. I urge you to have such conversations with your child throughout the summer. Explain your own beliefs and feelings about honor, integrity, and honesty. Review your own and the school's expectations about alcohol/drug use. Remind your child, above all, to be kind and accepting of others.

I would like to say that I included all of the above in my conversation with Brad prior to his leaving, but in hindsight, I honestly did not. Brad had a good idea of our values and our expectations of him. Moreover, while alcohol and drugs were intermittently discussed prior to his entering St. Andrew's, it was never a "sit down, let me talk to you" kind of discussion. I saved that conversation for his entrance into college; however, today I would recommend that parents have this conversation much earlier.

The handbook also included a yearly calendar outlining what one could expect throughout the year, including parents weekend, homecoming, trustee weekend, fall and spring examinations, and the beginning and end dates for each semester. Also outlined in the handbook were honor codes and information on counseling at St. Andrew's, student conduct, the alcohol/drug policy, hazing and harassment, discipline reports to colleges, the policy regarding sexual relationships between students, school leaves, transportation, chapel service, school debit cards, laundry, room furnishings, health services, and the dress code. Students were expected to dress appropriately. The boys wore sport jackets or blazers, collared shirts (ties during Wednesday evening dinner and Sunday chapel), and slacks or khakis. Girls wore dresses, skirts, or slacks with dress blouses and proper shoes. No athletic shoes, flip-flops, or shower shoes were allowed.

St. Andrew's did not allow students to have cars on campus without special permission from the dean. Keep in mind, this was a boarding school, not a boarding and *day* school combined.

There are, however, several schools of this kind that cater to both day and boarding school students. Occasionally, students from St. Andrew's, mainly seniors, were allowed to have cars on campus for special college weekend trips.

During our time, while visiting the potential schools, the head of school, at St. Andrew's had given a speech with several important points that had captured my interest in St. Andrew's. One such point had been his brief talk about students driving fancy cars on campus, which usually gave inference to the students, and/or parents' financial status. Tad Roach and other faculty members shunned that kind of conduct. He reminded us that St. Andrew's was a school that didn't just serve the wealthy and more privileged families, but *all* families. Tad Roach was sensitive to this type of thing, as portrayed in his writings, and he wanted students to feel they were always on an equal playing field, so to speak. Essentially, no group was better than another.

Later, as the school years progressed, I began to look forward to Tad Roach's writings (the "Head of School's Note") in the quarterly St. Andrew's magazine; although Brad has since graduated from St. Andrew's, I continue to look forward to reading this section. While I would like to include the entire column written by Tad Roach, which is often several pages long, here is an excerpt from a 2005 article titled "An Education for Life":

My greatest worry is that we might fail to grasp the opportunity for growth, learning, transformation, and inspiration that each class might provide. My worry is that you as individuals and as a school might settle for strategic learning and thinking instead of true immersion in the life of the mind. My worry is that you might treat your life, your relationship, your morality, your values, your principles as ones that are superficial, modest, and unambitious. I worry that you will fail to be exceptional because you fear that kind of effort, that kind of commitment, that kind of passion.

St. Andrew's is a learning and teaching academy, a school that has no qualms in asserting that your education is designed to inspire you to be active, moral agents in this country and the world. You are surrounded by teachers, scholars, a magnificent and accessible library, classes, and sections designed to engage you, pull you from the culture's passivity and mindlessness. Will you do the reading, thinking, questioning, analyzing, exploring that such an education requires and demands? Or will you succumb to the forces that pull you away from engagement, that make you a passive, even manipulative student? Will you encourage the engagement and intellectual commitment of your peers or join students in a conspiracy of indifference, apathy, and pretense?

Your very life depends on the way you answer that question. Or, to put it more precisely, the kind of person you become, the kind of citizen you become, the kind of leader you become depends on your willingness to open your mind and immerse yourself in the gift and glory of an education.

*   *   *

Students came from all over to attend St. Andrew's; most, however, were from the Virginia, Maryland, and Pennsylvania areas. A few were from New England and other areas of the United States or beyond our borders. Ethan Beringer, a boy who was in Brad's graduating class from St. Bernard's, came to St. Andrew's in his sophomore year instead of freshman year. His parents thought it best that Ethan finish the ninth grade at St. Bernard's. Whenever I bumped into his mother on my visits to the school, I was reminded that it may have been good for Brad to have waited until sophomore year, as his initial, freshman-year adjustment to St. Andrew's was a bit rocky.

Ethan appeared to have adjusted well, in spite of commonly held beliefs in the "boarding school world" that students often have difficulty adjusting to boarding school as latecomers. Again, entering during freshman year is the norm unless you are a transfer student.

A few years later, Nelson, an African American boy from one of the lower grades at St. Bernard's, came to St. Andrew's as a freshman and joined Brad and Ethan.

Peter Wong's last letter to me confirmed Brad's difficulty adjusting to this new environment. The first year had been rough for Brad. I had considered removing him from St. Andrew's after an incident the first year that had appeared to take the form of hazing. In fact, not knowing what else to do, I had called George School to see if it were possible for Brad to transfer there since he had already been accepted and we were familiar with the school.

When Brad came home a few weeks later in the spring, he, Al, and I had a meeting, which did not turn out as I had expected. Brad insisted on going back to St. Andrew's, and Al agreed. Al sided with Brad and said I was making too much of the incident and that there was no need to transfer Brad from St. Andrew's. Nevertheless, I was concerned about Brad's return. I was also surprised by the lack of support from Al. The next day, I placed a call to Peter Wong's home. Peter did not mind parents contacting him at his home; in fact, he encouraged parents to do so. We talked for a long while; Peter suggested that Brad return to the school and assured me that he would monitor the situation closely and remain in constant contact with me and Mitchell Beam, who was the corridor monitor for the upcoming term. Mitchell Beam was also Brad's history teacher. Peter asked that I remain in continuous contact with him as the year progressed.

Brad returned to St. Andrew's, but before he left, I talked with him about his sporadic calls to me and his dad and reminded him that he should call more regularly. We did, however, instant message quite often; we used that method of communicating instead of emails. I also talked about his responsibility to inform me immediately if something should happen. Over the next several years, Brad appeared to adjust quite well.

21.

MONTHLY VISITS HOME:
ANTICIPATION! PARENT CONFERENCES AND THEATER AND SPORTING EVENTS

I never dreamed about success, I worked for it.

—Estée Lauder

All students were allowed to go home once every month. They would leave on Friday afternoon after classes and return to St. Andrew's on Sunday evening. Some students were picked up by their parents, while others took the shuttle to buses hired by St. Andrew's, to be dropped off in various locations including busy downtown New York, near Penn Station. The parents picked up their children from there. Most of the time, I was so excited to see Brad that I would arrive an hour before the bus was scheduled to arrive. I would sit in my car waiting in a no-parking zone in front of the main post office on 33rd Street, accompanied by a line of other cars. Most times, I was shooed away by the waving hand of a police officer or meter attendant. I would drive around the block a couple of times and, given the traffic, could easily take fifteen minutes or so to return to the same spot.

When Brad finally arrived, we would make plans to do something fun that day; we might see a movie or have a meal at a favorite restaurant, either in the city or closer to home. Whatever it was, I'd try to leave the decision up to him.

During Brad's first year at St. Andrew's, I refinanced the condominium where we lived in the Bronx, rented it out, and moved up to Peekskill, New York. Peekskill is one of the last towns in Westchester County, so the drive was long, about one hour and twenty minutes from midtown Manhattan.

The long drive was a blessing! I discovered that the best time to gather information from a child was when they were held captive in a car with no place to go. Brad was sometimes talkative, but most of the time he was not. He would submerge himself in one of the computer magazines that he purchased along the way, deliberately ignoring my questions.

I discovered, though, that if my questions were of a social nature, as opposed to "How is your science class going?" he was more than willing to engage in conversation. For example, if I asked, "What's Daniel up to lately? Or Kyle?" or one of his other friends, then he loved to give me updates. Daniel was going home with one of the other classmates for the spring break, or another friend's big sister was getting married, or one of the parents had visited and taken them all out to dinner— he'd turn into a chatterbox.

Even today, Brad gives updates on most of his friends or former roommates, who usually became friends. Friendships were and still are important to him. I suspect Brad is a good friend to others, as they appear to be with him. Many times, this is a prerequisite to good friendships that last throughout the years. Brad is the kind of a person who is supportive and comes to your aid if you need him. He has a kind spirit, and people are usually drawn to him.

*   *   *

Parents weekend was scheduled a couple of times throughout the school year; although those weekends were set up for parent-teacher conferences, it also allowed for social interaction between parents, students, administrators, and faculty. These special weekends began on Friday evening and ended late Sunday afternoon. Parents had the option to either arrive on Friday evening to attend a St. Andrew's play, performed by students of the theater department, or arrive Saturday morning. The plays were quite professional, with professionally built props and genuinely good acting.

I usually went up alone on Friday evening, and Al would come Saturday morning, sometimes with Hannah and Parker. I rented a motel room close to the school. Brad and I called it the "Bates Motel." It had an eerie, barren look with no greenery and looked as if a tumbleweed might roll by at any moment. Occasionally, during the winter months, when it got dark early, I would arrive at night. The office would be dimly lit, and an older man or woman would shuffle to the counter to help me. Then I would be reminded of where to drop the keys off when I checked out. Quite a few of the parents stayed at the "Bates" because it was close to the school. However, as we got more familiar with the surroundings, we would go to Dover or the next town over. Sometimes when my mother came to Delaware with me, we would stay at one of the nicer hotels in either of the towns.

On Saturday morning, the parents were provided a schedule of events and a list of the designated classrooms where the parent-teacher conferences would be held. The parents were accompanied to the classrooms by their sons or daughters. When the conferences ended around noon, the parents then gathered in the theaterw for welcoming remarks from the head of school.

Following lunch, there was a series of outdoor games. Brad played soccer, one of his favorite sports. Other games included volleyball, football, lacrosse, and crew. St. Andrew's was situated by a very large lake, and crew was one of its most prized sports.

On Sunday, all were expected to attend chapel services, which were followed by a jazz concert and choir and more parent-teacher conferences, if you had not had a chance to meet with the teachers on Saturday morning.

The day ended about 3:00 p.m., and a feeling of emptiness would accompany me on my drive home.

22.

PLAN FOR COLLEGE ADMISSIONS PROCESS

When we seek to discover the best in others,
we somehow bring out the best in ourselves.
—*William Arthur Ward*

In preparation for the college admissions process, the College Counseling office asked parents to provide information about each child. An excerpt from their letter went as follows: "We invite you to share your personal perspective as well as anecdotal highlights of your child's past four years encompassing summer activities, previous schooling, or involvement in your home community. This is your opportunity to be proud, honest, funny, or serious as well as share those thoughts that you hope college admissions officers will understand about your child."

I responded with this:

Brad is a highly intelligent individual with a sense of humor, along with a serious purpose. Academically, Brad has a fine mind. His problem-solving, understanding, and quick processing skills are sometimes astonishing. He possesses strong mathematical skills and the ability to manipulate numbers. Even as a young child, simple math and other concepts were easy for Brad to grasp. Science, another strong area for Brad, was something he grew to enjoy over time.

At a very early age, Brad was trained in computer technology by his father. While he was in a C++ class at St. Andrew's, the teacher commented that Brad was so competent in this area that all he had to do was put a computer in front of Brad and he would be proficient at programming it on his own.

As a youngster, Brad was encouraged, to some degree, to make decisions of his own. As he began to age, we continued to encourage this, sometimes offering suggestions where needed. As a result, Brad developed good decision-making skills. There is, for the most part, a level of trust that leads us to believe he will continue to make good decisions. And, of course, being away from home in a boarding school setting has fostered this.

While Brad has little hesitation when making decisions, on occasions he procrastinates in putting them in action—usually with an assuredness that he can get his desired task done, even at the eleventh hour.

In Brad's first five years of schooling, he was tested and placed in an exceptionally gifted class in the public school system. The work was quite demanding and required end-of-month assignments. Since the assignments were given at the beginning of each month, Brad was encouraged to do a little at a time to build on their completion. Well, with much prodding, the assignments would get done. This is not to say, however, that Brad preferred to be out and about playing. He is primarily a home-bodied individual who would typically be at his computer or reading. As Brad approached fifth grade and started at St. Bernard's, St. Bernard's had an end-of-day required study hall as part of their curriculum. Brad was now very much aware of what had to get done. Even on days when he attended away games, he would arrive home in the evenings, often-times exhausted, eat, and immediately start on his homework.

Brad reads a great deal, primarily magazines. Our home is loaded with back issues of *Popular Science* maga-zines. Brad has asked to have the subscribed issues sent to St. Andrew's. However, knowing the potential for distraction, we kept the magazines at home for his reading pleasure. Also, in hindsight, if Brad were able to purchase *every* computer magazine on the newsstand, he would. On numerous occasions, he has used the last of his allowance to purchase two or three computer magazines at a given time.

Brad has a strong competitive nature, much of which stems from participating in a variety of sports. Over the years, he has played soccer, lacrosse (he was captain of JV lacrosse) basketball, tennis, and baseball. Competitive sports are taken very seriously. Once, before a visit to St. Andrew's, Brad and I had discussed the need to purchase a suit for the prom. He was very excited about this (he had not owned a suit since third grade and had for the most part lived in khakis and blazers). Well, when Brad discovered he had an away game and there would be a schedule conflict regarding the time available to purchase the suit, he was very clear about his priorities. The suit had to take the back seat. "The team needs me," he commented. According to reports received from St. Andrew's, Brad has a good attitude and an even temperament and has developed into a valuable member of the team. Next year, Brad is expected to contribute as a player at the varsity level in all of his current sports.

Academically, we have encouraged Brad to channel his competitive nature to compete on his own merit. He has always been very concerned about his grades, including his PSAT and now SAT scores. For example, he voluntarily repeated the SAT to obtain a score that represented his best effort. This past year, Brad had very demanding classes, including two honors courses and Advanced Placement courses. He again showed solid academic performance and a cumulative average well within the honors range. In addition, Brad was honored with the National Latin Examination Award (summa cum laude). Toward the close of his junior year, we discussed, along with Brad's advisor, the classes he would take in his senior year. Of course, knowing the demands of the college admissions process, concerns were raised with regards to his enrollment in advanced physics, potentially a very demanding class, to say the least. Yet his discipline usually demonstrated his commitment to success. We are confident that Brad will rise to the challenge and prioritize where needed.

Brad is an only child of divorced parents. However, he has a brother and two sisters from his dad's previous marriages, with whom he is very close. It is probably because of these relationships that he is sensitive and very respectful of the privacy of others. His sensitivity has always prompted him to come to the aid of others.; he does not take a passive role. Brad has also developed solid leadership skills and has earned respect among his peers; this past year, Brad was elected as junior class vice president. In addition, while visiting St. Andrew's, I have witnessed on a few occasions classmates have popped into his room to ask questions on various subjects. If he knew the answer, Brad would provide it without hesitation.

In sum, Brad is bright, good-natured, an enthusiastic student, and interested in the world around him. We are very proud and trust that he will confidently welcome any challenges put forth to him and rise to meet them successfully.

Having written this rather lengthy and well-deserved praise about Brad, I asked the secretary at my place of employment if she would be kind enough to proof the document for me. She read the material and commented, "Gee, you really think very highly of Brad."

I responded with a smile and said, "Yes, I do, Karen, and I hope you think the same about your boys, for each person has their own unique gifts."

Karen was a young mother of four boys. While she loved them dearly, one day, shortly after our talk, she confided in me that once she returned home from work and prepared dinner each evening, she retreated to her computer to avoid interaction with them. I have since encouraged Karen to spend time observing her boys for their individual potential and to explore a variety of avenues by which to educate them.

23.

COLLEGE ADMISSIONS PROCESS: DEADLINES? NO EXCEPTIONS!

A life spent making mistakes is not only more honorable,
but more useful than a life spent doing nothing.
—George Bernhard Shaw

Brad began the college application process. Accepted to leading Ivy League schools, he chose Princeton University and majored in electrical engineering. I kept copies of all of the acceptance letters and put them in a binder to have as a keepsake.

St. Andrew's was very involved in the process of making certain all deadlines were on course, while giving students breathing room. Students were busy filling out applications, writing essays, and answering questions; no applications, questions, or essays were the same or even similar, so none could be reused. The college application process was demanding, with a universal deadline like income taxes—all applications had to be postmarked by January 1st. No exceptions whatsoever!

I recall that Brad and I argued the day prior to the application submission deadline—he was still a procrastinator and last-minute with many things. To my surprise, though, whatever it was, it always appeared to get done. Nonetheless, when it came to something as important as a deadline, his penchant for procrastination always kept me on edge.

On this day, Brad was at Hannah's apartment in mid-Manhattan, completing the essays, applications, etc. She lived not far from the major post office on 8th Avenue and 33rd Street. Brad was scheduled to come home to Peekskill that evening, but I pleaded with him to wrap it up and mail the application packet from the post office there, because of the threat of a major snowstorm in Peekskill. Fortunately, he followed my advice, because the next day we were buried under snow; no cars could move. Had he waited, he would have missed the deadline for submission. Remember: no exceptions!

Today, thankfully, many college application requirements are online submissions.

*   *   *

In the spring of 2001, Brad graduated from St. Andrew's with honors and was the recipient of several awards. It was an exceptionally beautiful day. The joy of having lots of family join us for the celebration was peerless! In the years since that momentous occasion, St. Andrew's continues to engage its alumni, parents, faculty, and friends for one night each year by hosting worldwide gatherings to honor the "great spirit" of St. Andrew's. The gatherings consist of groups of varying sizes, and are either held in someone's home or a larger venue for what is referred to as the "Coast to Coast Toasts.". Some of the locations have included Boston; San Francisco; Taipei, Taiwan; Shanghai, China; North Carolina; and Toronto, Ontario. This annual fellowship helps to spread goodwill among students and keeps them connected and engaged. Brad remains in contact with some of his graduating class, faculty, and staff.

*   *   *

The school year passed swiftly. After graduation, our schedules often included a variety of events, and family time appeared to become increasingly significant for us as we prepared for Brad's move to another state for college in early fall. As summer waned, Brad decided to accompany his dad to Virginia to visit with his paternal grandmother and elder sister.

He was becoming a young man now; therefore, some of our leisure time was spent differently. Still, both Brad and I loved to eat out occasionally. Sometimes, when I picked him up from school, we would go to a local Italian restaurant and order our favorite eggplant or shrimp Parmesan. We had gotten used to eating this dish because Al was a pescatarian. Not a vegetarian, as Al would sometimes refer to himself, but a pescatarian; we enjoyed our fish and seafood dishes. One of our very favorite restaurants was the Windows on the World, located in the *then* World Trade Center. Some Sundays, Alice and her son, Santiago, Brad, and I would have a delicious brunch buffet there on the 107th floor of the North Tower building. The kids especially loved the ride on the elevator, which appeared to take less than fifteen seconds from point A to point B. Without a doubt, the view from the top was spectacular! While we were married, Al and I had also sometimes frequented the Chrysler Building or Windows on the World for dinner in the evenings. The view was even more charming at night, while overlooking the city lights. Oh! What we take for granted. We had never suspected a tragedy like 9/11 would happen. The world was devastated!

I vividly remember that day. Brad had just left for his first year at Princeton a few days prior, and I was at work in the Bronx. I was employed as a director for a nonprofit program with a staff of nine. The bookkeeper, who sometimes struggled with his English, stayed in the recreation room watching the television as the entire horrific event unfolded. The rest of us gathered in my office, and he would come in intermittently to provide us with updates. The last time he visited, almost in tears and very excited, he informed us that the first tower had fallen. We looked at one another, barely understanding the bookkeeper's quivering voice, which switched between both English and Spanish. Initially we all thought he was kidding. We then followed him to watch the television; paralyzed by the news and in dismay, we couldn't take our eyes off the screen. I cannot remember if Brad called me first, or if I called him. The telephone landlines were hardly operable with everyone trying to get through. Those of us who had cell phones were slightly better off. Brad called his dad and siblings and tried to reach his grandmother, who had a landline. He was especially concerned for his sister Hannah, who was now an ER doctor and was working at one of the nearby hospitals in Manhattan. He knew she would more than likely be on the front lines, assisting the injured. We were all nervous and in shock.

That weekend, I stayed in my pajamas, watching the late Peter Jennings and other newscasters as they reported the news, perhaps also while in disbelief. On the following Monday, as I was leaving Peekskill for work, I drove past the Metro North, a commuter train station, where I saw the same cars that had been parked there the day of this tragedy and that had remained there for a number of days thereafter. I wondered if those poor souls had perished.

At work, it was *not* business as usual. We were all somber; the atmosphere was different. One of the staff members, Ronald, did not come to work or call. We were concerned. He eventually came in a few days later, stating he and some of his friends had been in search of one of their close friends, who worked at the World Trade Center. As it turned out, his friend was found, had been slightly injured, and was at the point of an emotional breakdown. We were just glad Ronald was okay; I embraced him when he walked into my office, and the rest of the team did likewise.

The following weekend, I felt I needed to help in some way. I was on edge thinking about Brad alone, away from home, and how he may have continued to worry about us. Remembering how, when he had left for boarding school, the tragedy of Princess Diana, had occurred the night before his departure, I was troubled. How does one rest or concentrate on their schoolwork in the face of tragedy? Studying engineering was tough enough already, to say the least.

My need to help and to take my mind off of Brad led me to the local Salvation Army in Peekskill. There, I volunteered to put together packages—water and the like—to be sent down to Ground Zero for the hundreds of volunteers. It was a very exhilarating and exhausting day, but worth every second and more.

9/11 appeared to change everything! On some days, my paranoia would get the best of me. I refused to go to any meetings in Manhattan. I feared for those I knew, both family and friends who lived in tall high-rise buildings. Also, while before I had flown many places, I now refused to fly. I would drive over the George Washington Bridge, all the while praying I'd make it to the other side. I would get stuck in traffic on the Cross Bronx Expressway, I-95, which was always at a standstill in a certain areas of the highway, and I would pray the traffic would break so I could get to my destination.

Most of all, my paranoia kept gnawing at me as I thought of Brad and wondered if the attackers might target the schools housing what some may consider the "best and the brightest": Harvard, Yale, Princeton, MIT, Stanford, and so on. In my mind, this is how a terrorist would think; wipe out America's next generation of the young and most intelligent. Fortunately, none of it has come to fruition. Life changed, yet life went on.

*   *   *

Although this book was written through the eyes of my own experiences educating my *now*-adult son, its purpose is to motivate and arm you, the reader, with well-researched information, as well as to encourage you to become more actively involved in the education of your children. Students can and will learn countless things of value in school, yet many can also become uninterested and disengaged before discovering the authentic joy of learning. The love of learning is a privilege. I have attempted to open a clear pathway by providing a bird's-eye view of the rights a parent of a public school student has and to provide an alternative path one could take: a *private independent school education*. I have committed to emphasizing the latter.

It is my honor to encourage you to say "yes" as you also invite others to assist in increasing the ranks of truly concerned parents who desire the best educational experiences for their children. Meaningful change can be instrumental in impacting not only the lives of countless individuals now, but also future generations as this commitment is nurtured and unfolds. If you decide to apply to an *independent private school* (day or boarding) on your own or through a supportive program specifically designed to guide you through the entire process from start to finish, it will be your choice. Good luck!

24.

ELEVATE YOUR COMFORT LEVEL: AN INVALUABLE RESOURCE GUIDE

Tell me and I forget.

Teach me and I remember.

Involve me and I learn.

—Benjamin Franklin

HELPFUL ORGANIZATIONS AND WEBSITES

The Parents League of New York

In addition to my friend Alice's suggestions, the Parents League of New York was my go-to source for information. At the time, the League only provided a printed hard copy that listed neighboring, private independent day schools in NYC, as well as boarding schools in New York and other states. Since computers were not as ubiquitous during the time we were applying as they are now, obtaining an online list of schools was not an option. Today, the Parents League still provides hard copies for distribution at school fairs, but the digital option is the preferred method used by members of the Parents League to access a list of schools.

The Parents League of New York is affiliated with 300 member schools from pre-K through twelfth grade. The dues for family membership are currently $315 annually. Members receive ongoing guidance from those who are knowledgeable in the industry, which allows parents to make the most informed decisions for their children and for their family. The parents also receive unlimited one-on-one meetings, as well as unlimited follow-up phone calls, emails, pre-school admissions workshops, and continued support throughout the entire admissions process. For more information about the Parents League of New York and a list of schools, please visit: parentsleague.org or call (212) 737-7385.

Throughout the United States, there are organizations similar to the Parents League of New York that focus on independent private schools and assist parents along the complex path of locating the schools that are most suitable for their children. I have listed some very helpful organizations that will assist you in navigating the process according to region.

National Association of Independent Schools (NAIS)

The National Association of Independent Schools (NAIS) is a nonprofit organization that represents 1,900-plus member schools, both nationally and abroad. This includes approximately 1,600 independent private day/boarding K–12 schools in the United States. The mission of the NAIS is to serve as the voice of independent schools and preserve the independence of the schools while also ensuring that the process provides quality and serves as a catalyst for innovation, improvement, and excellence. For a school to become a member of the NAIS, the school must have operated for at least five years and must be accredited by an accrediting organization approved by the NAIS.

The NAIS website carries a list of all its member schools.

You may obtain a list of independent schools of interest using the NAIS website:

- www.nais.org.
- At the top of the page, click **Directories**, then click **Find a School**.
- Using the filtering options in the navigation bar on the right, refine schools by **School Type** (Day, Boarding, or Boarding Day), below see **Region** (e.g., East-NJ/NY, Middle Atlantic, DE/DC, Mid West, etc.), **Grade Levels**, **Student Body** (Boys, Girls, or Coed), and more.
- Click on your school of choice and you will see a brief synopsis of the school as well as the admissions person to contact.

Association of Independent Schools in New England (AISNE)

This organization serves students and families in the New England area (Massachusetts, Maine, New Hampshire, Rhode Island, and Vermont). For more information, visit: aisne.org or call (617) 329-1483.

Puget Sound Independent Schools (PSIS)

Self-described as an admissions collaborative connecting families and schools, this organization serves students and families in the Seattle, Washington area. For more information, visit: pugetsoundindependentschools.org.

New Jersey Association of Independent Schools (NJAIS)

This organization serves New Jersey-area schools. For information, please visit: njais.org or call (888) 472-3491.

East Bay Independent Schools Association (EBISA)

EBISA offers help in the California Bay Area. For more information, visit: issfba.org. Go to **Schools**, search by **Region**.

Connecticut Association of Independent Schools (CAIS)

This organization offers guidance on Connecticut-area schools. For more information, visit caisct.org.

Georgia Independent School Association (GISA)

The association helps with Georgia-area schools. For more information, visit gisaschools.org or call (706) 938-1400.

NICHE

I found NICHE to be one of the most comprehensive and helpful organizations—very similar to the NAIS. Formerly known as the College Prowler, it is a broad-based company that runs a national ranking and review website to aid students and families in choosing colleges. It has now expanded to K–12 schools and offers information connecting schools and colleges with students and their families. The site's database and search engine help millions of students and families throughout the United States sort through information to find the right school, including private, independent schools.

NICHE is a great tool. It provides lists of schools and also offers detailed information about the schools as well as information on their ratings (how the school ranks among its peers), academics, tuition, culture, diversity, and reviews. The reviews themselves can be very helpful. The schools are rated based on key statistics from students and their families. The data comes from surveys, reviews, and other public data sources, and it is constantly reevaluated to make certain the information provides a comprehensive profile and is up-to-date and accurate.

For more information, please visit niche.com. Click K–12 and, in the search bar at the top of the page, type the state or city desired and navigate from there.

OTHER SUPPORTIVE PROGRAMS

In addition to the organizations listed above, there are supportive programs that prepare students for entry into independent day/boarding schools like the aforementioned *Early Steps, Prep for Prep,* and *A Better Chance Program.* Several sources are available to empower underserved, high-achieving minority students in a variety of regions; make contact and receive.

Prep for Prep

Brad's friend Paul, whom he met in middle school and who had gone through the Prep for Prep program, proudly offered to assist in filling in the gaps in my preparation of the material about the program for this book. After I mentioned to Paul that I had managed to pull some of the information off the Prep for Prep website, he assured me that I had only scratched the surface of what the program truly offered in its richness and depth. This program, as Paul explained it, had helped him in so many other areas of his life. He spoke of how Prep for Prep had broadened his way of thinking and prepared him to see life differently, benefits that he and his parents would never have anticipated.

In preparing this material, my aim is not to overburden the reader with unessential details but instead to provide a helpful overview of the Prep for Prep program, other similar programs offered, and how one can streamline an otherwise daunting process. The information should assist the reader in deciding if these avenues are appropriate for their son or daughter.

Prep for Prep was founded in 1978 to address the needs of the underrepresented segment of young people who possessed leadership potential. The program is designed for talented students from minority-group backgrounds who are prepared for placement in independent schools, both at the middle and high school levels. Each year, 3,500 or more city-wide students who demonstrate strong academic ability, participate in the talent search. One of the 750 or more participating New York City public elementary and junior high schools nominate top students. The selection process generally results in the admissions of ninety-five fifth graders and thirty sixth graders who enter the Prep for Prep program and are then placed in independent day schools in the seventh and eighth grades. Sixty seventh graders are also selected and enter the PREP 9 program. Prep for Prep prepares students for entrance into independent boarding high schools that serve the tristate area, including Westchester, Long Island, New Jersey, and Connecticut.

The Nomination Process: In order to identify candidates for Prep for Prep, school principals generally nominate students or selection is made at the recommendation of teachers and/or guidance counselors who feel the candidates have leadership qualities and are looked upon as potential leaders of tomorrow. The program maintains an ongoing relationship with both teachers and guidance counselors from the participating schools. After a student is selected, they must mentally prepare themselves to commit to a fourteen-month course of study including two intensive seven-week summer sessions, as well as one day a week after school and all-day Saturday classes during the school year. Prep for Prep also maintains ongoing contact with each student as part of their commitment.

Here are a few Frequently Asked Questions (FAQs):

What is the success rate of students who are admitted to Prep for Prep?

According to Prep for Prep statistics, at least 75% of the students who begin the fourteen-month intensive academic preparatory study successfully complete it.

Are all students who are in Prep admitted to independent schools?

There is a strong partnership between Prep for Prep and the independent schools that participate. It is the expectation of the program that every child who remains in good standing will be admitted to one of the eighty-plus participating independent schools; however, each independent school will make the final decision on a particular candidate.

Who determines which independent school a child will attend?

The parent and the child will make the ultimate decision if given a choice of schools; however, in the actual selection process, the Prep for Prep staff provides counseling to recommend schools which are suitable for the candidate. This usually involves a student applying to two or three schools after having visited them.

How about the financial aid process?

Students who are admitted to independent schools are guaranteed financial aid to the extent that each student's family warrants it. Each family situation is analyzed individually by the Student Services for Financial Aid and the independent school. The formula for the aid takes into consideration family income as well as a variety of factors which may affect a family's ability to contribute toward the student's education expenses. According to Prep for Prep statistics, many of the families qualify for full-tuition aid awards or close to full-tuition awards. The premise, however, is that each family is responsible for the costs of education for its children to the extent they are able to pay; financial aid is designed to make up the difference.

What happens post-placement?

Once a student enters the independent school, Prep for Prep continues to support, nurture, and offer individual counseling to them. Every month, the students can expect a visit from an assigned Prep Counselor to offer assistance where needed. Additionally, every Saturday, the students involve themselves in recreation, for example, excursions to sporting events and cultural activities that include skiing and visits to the Liberty Science Center, the Franklin-Institute, plays, movies, and picnics, etc.

Prep for Prep advises students on college entrance (preparation for the SAT exam, application submission, and financial aid), serves as an advocate with the colleges on behalf of the students, and arranges for students to visit the schools.

A sample list of independent schools participating in the Prep for Prep and PREP 9 program:

DAY SCHOOLS

Allen-Stevenson
Bank Street
Berkeley Carroll
Brearley
BrooklynFriends
Browning
Buckley School
Calhoun
Cathedral
Chapin
Collegiate
Columbia Prep
Dalton
Fieldston
Friends
Hackley
Hewitt
Horace Mann
ManhattanCountry
Marymount
Nightingale-Bamford
Packer-Collegiate
Poly Prep Country Day
Riverdale Country
Sacred Heart

Saint David's
St. Ann's
St. Bernard's
Spence
Staten Island Academy
Town
Trevor Day
Trinity
Village Community
York Prep
*Other schools

Boarding Schools
Prep 9 Consortium Schools
Andove
Choate
Deerfield
Exeter
Hotchkiss
Lawrenceville
Middlesex
Milton
St. Andrew's
Taft

The Prep for Prep community includes over 5,000 students and alumni. For more information, please visit: prepforprep. org or call (212) 579-1470 or (212) 579-1390.

EARLY STEPS

Need creating need . . . a program fostering racial diversity in independent schools.

The Early Steps program was created as a resource to address the needs of families of color living in New York City (and Long Island) who were seeking a quality education for their children. At the same time, independent schools were seeking to racially diversify their student populations.

Unlike Prep for Prep, Early Steps works specifically with families whose children are entering kindergarten or first grade. They offer guidance during the admissions process to include information about school visits and interviews, guidance on the ERB (Education Records Bureau) testing process, and assistance with admissions and financial aid applications. Many participating/member schools of the Early Steps program have varying characteristics, including location, teaching style, and whether they are coed, all-boys, or all-girls schools. This program helps families according to their particular needs and preferences.

Financial Assistance (F/A) Early Steps provides counseling and support to families applying for financial assistance that "represent a broad range of income levels," according to their website. While some receive financial aid in varying amounts, other Early Steps families do not need financial assistance and pay the tuition in full. The financial process is primarily the same as the Prep for Prep program. The Student Services for Financial Aid organization is utilized as a resource by most, if not all, independent schools to determine family need. Again, the formula takes into account not only family income but also a variety of factors which may affect a family's ability to contribute toward the child's education.

As most are aware, independent schools are tuition-based, and their fees vary greatly. The school determines and makes all financial aid grants to the student. Early Steps does *not* provide financial assistance to families; however, the program does provide counseling and guidance to families applying for financial assistance. Financial assistance is also contingent upon the independent school's available resources.

How to get started: When your child turns four for kindergarten or five for first grade, contact Early Steps for an application. From there, your child will be guided through the entire application and ERB testing process. Please visit: early-steps.org or Contact Early Step by emailing earlysteps@early-steps.org or calling (212) 288-9684.

A Better Chance (ABC)

A Better Chance program was founded in 1963 for students of color. This program is nationwide and prepares students for entrance into college prep private and select public schools. To qualify, students must be in grades four through nine, rank in the top 10 percent of their class, demonstrate leadership potential, and have good character. The program currently has 2,000-plus students enrolled in approximately 350 private day and/

or boarding schools as well as some of the best public schools throughout the country.

While the majority of students in this program are African American, today the program embraces a diverse student population, including those with varying economic backgrounds—not only those in financial need, but also middle-class and upper-middle-class families.

Similar to the Prep for Prep program, ABC students are expected to adopt a rigorous academic schedule. The first four months are devoted to the application process and information sessions. During the following fourteen months, the candidate goes through intense workshops, including mock interviews and training on essay writing, standardized testing (ISEE/SSAT exams), and financial aid awareness.

A Better Chance begins to look for the best fit for the student as they finalize the application process. ABC evaluates the student's overall profile to determine which schools the student should be referred to; at this point, the student then begins the interviewing process. ABC advocates with the member schools on behalf of the students. As previously mentioned, while the student and parents will make the ultimate decision if given a choice of schools, each school will make the final decision on a particular candidate. A Better Chance has a strong alumni base, with over 16,000 alumni, many of whom are influential in the disciplines of government, education, business, medicine, and the arts. ABC's national office is headquartered in New York City but serves nationwide. For more information and to apply, please visit: www.abetterchance.org or by email admissions@abetterchance.org or call (646) 346-1310.

Independent School Alliance

This organization serves students and families of color in grades K–9 in the Los Angeles area. Prospective students must demonstrate school readiness for kindergarten or for the grade they are entering. School records and test scores must be strong for referral to the program and thus entrance into a member independent school.

The Independent Alliance supports families and the students admitted to the nine-month program in preparation and navigation through the independent school admissions process. The program charges a consultation fee, and the parent is responsible for any additional fees such as exam fees and financial aid application fees. For more information, please visit: independentschoolalliance.org or, for questions email: mail to:info@independentschoolalliance.org or call (213) 484-2411.

REACH Prep

Serving Connecticut (Fairfield County), Westchester, and the Bronx, this program admits fourth-grade students into a rigorous fifteen-month course of study intended to prepare students for admissions to an independent middle schools .Today, REACH Prep provides 250-plus students each year with exceptional opportunities to develop the skills and motivation necessary to become effective leaders. For more information, please visit: reachprep.org or call (203) 487-0750.

High Jump

This program serves middle school students (sixth graders) of diverse backgrounds in the Chicago, Illinois, area. The students are selected based on their capability to excel academically, and the program targets those who are highly motivated and who simply enjoy learning. Participating students have high academic potential but are challenged by limited opportunities and resources. At High Jump, the students engage in a rigorous two-year course of study. They are provided with an academic enrichment program with the goal of preparing students to enter independent schools and other college preparatory schools, as well as colleges. For more information, visit: highjumpchicago.org or call (312) 582-7700.

Queen City Foundation

This program serves the Cincinnati, Ohio, area, providing a highly enriched program to minority students from grades six to eight and nine to twelve in preparation for admission to independent schools, both day and boarding. The Queen City Foundation actively seeks academically motivated and talented students to enter the program. Their vision is to provide support, a solid academic program, and exposure to resources that will prepare students to become productive, creative, and engaged leaders of tomorrow. For more information, visit: queencity foundation.org, or email qcfeducation@gmail.com, or call (513) 655-5402.

Oliver Scholars

Unlocking opportunities for underserved Black and Latino students, this program serves in a unique position in the New York City area. Oliver Scholars accepts applications from high-achieving, top-of-their-class seventh graders who demonstrate the academic, social, and leadership skills necessary to thrive in an independent school environment. Students may be nominated by teachers, counselors or, if highly motivated, themselves.

Nominations are necessary in order for a student to receive an invitation for admission to Oliver Scholars. Similar to Prep for Prep, the student is immersed in a rigorous, supportive fourteen-month program. The supports provided by the program are such that the student realizes their full potential and ultimately is prepared to give back to the city, the nation, and the world. Most are placed in top independent schools and later attend and graduate Ivy League or highly selective colleges. For more information, please visit: oliverscholars.org, or call (212) 430-5980.

Baltimore Educational Scholarship Trust (B.E.S.T.)

Serving the Baltimore, Maryland, area, this program enrolls African American students in grades K–9. Potential students must be high achievers and demonstrate above-average standardized test scores. The student does *not* have to be nominated, but parents are encouraged to answer the questions proposed on the B.E.S.T. website to help determine if the rigorous course-work necessary to enter into an independent school environment is a good fit for the child.

Once accepted to the program, students are positioned for success through academic preparation, and character and leadership development. As with the aforementioned programs, the students are supported throughout the application process while applying to member independent schools. For more information, visit: besttrust.org or call (410) 752-2225.

Steppingstones Scholars

This program offers opportunities to underserved students in the Philadelphia, Pennsylvania, area. The program prepares and nurtures high-achieving students in fifth through twelfth grades through summer internships and weekend sessions or, depending on the grade level, a rigorous fourteen-month program leading to placement in an independent school. Nominations are required for entrance into the program. For more information, visit: steppingstonescholars.org or call (215) 204-5130.

Fund for Advancement of Minorities (FAME)

FAME provides talented minority students access to an independent school education in the Greater Pittsburgh, Pennsylvania area through summer and weekend enrichment opportunities. Their goal is to empower and increase the number of minority students who wish to become leaders of tomorrow. Support is provided throughout the students' academic career. For more information, visit: famefund.org or call (412) 363-5553.

The Steppingstone Foundation

Serving the Boston, Massachusetts, area and historically marginalized communities, the foundation operates *three* programs: **TSA** (Steppingstone Academy) prepares middle-grade students for admissions to top independent schools, Catholic schools, and high-achieving public schools. Students must complete a rigorous fourteen-month academic program. After enrolling in their new schools, the students receive continued support to ensure they graduate from high school as well as college. Nomination to the TSA program is required. **CSA** (College Success Academy) offers guidance to public school students in grades K through 8, and the **NPEA** (the National Partnership for Educational Access), a member organization, seeks to remove barriers to educational access for approximately 500,000 underserved students nationwide. For more information, visit: tsf.org or call (617) 423-6300.

TEAK Fellowship—Transforming Lives. Lifting Communities.

TEAK is a full, comprehensive program serving low-income middle school–age students in the New York City area. The program attracts high-achieving *sixth graders* who demonstrates a 90% academic average or above and are nominated by teachers. There is a selection process for finalists that includes an admissions exam as well as an interview. Although TEAK serves middle school children, it is a ten-year, exceptionally supportive program, helping students from middle school through college. Most participants attend and graduate Ivy League or other highly selective colleges.

This robust enrichment program provides guidance and support, consisting of rigorous five full days of academic studies during the summers, usually from July through August. The program also offers an after-school program twice per week and an additional class one Saturday each month for the seventh and eighth graders. Once students successfully advance through middle school, they continue to adopt a rigorous academic schedule which then *prepares them for admission to the most selective high schools—the next milestone.*

With the assistance of a placement counselor, eighth-grade students advancing to high school may choose one of the four types of schools listed as follows:

- Independent Private *Day* Schools
- Independent Private *Boarding* Schools
- Screened High Schools (specialized and sought-after high schools in the NYC area)
- Parochial Schools

The choice in the selection of schools is up to individual families.

Students remain at their respective schools through eighth grade and attend the TEAK classes at separate locations in four of the five boroughs. However, students are selected from all five boroughs, including Staten Island.

Classroom sizes are small, twelve to sixteen students—modeling a private school atmosphere and a better learning environment. Some students become a part of the TEAK community because they don't feel sufficiently challenged at their current schools. The TEAK curriculum is of an advanced level, providing students with the multifaceted opportunities they need for growth.

TEAK is *free* and does not cost families anything. In addition to its highly supportive environment, the program is committed to assisting families in getting familiar with a variety of high schools and eventually colleges. The support also includes tours to boarding schools, addressing the families' financial needs and the preparation of financial aid forms, and guidance on the college admissions process, among other services. For more

information, please visit: teakfellowship.org, email admissions@
teakfellowship.org regarding admissions, or call (212) 288-6678.

Breakthrough Collaborative—Building Bridges in Communities.

Breakthrough, headquartered in Oakland, California, serves
students of diverse backgrounds who are traditionally underrepresented and are from under-resourced communities. This
nationwide program adopts a similar viewpoint to many of the
other programs addressed in this section: that every child deserves
a quality education regardless of economic access or privilege.

The program begins in middle school—sixth graders and
rising seventh, eighth, and ninth graders—and continues for
six or more years, providing support throughout. Students are
expected to adhere to a rigorous program that prepares them
for college and further.

The goal of Breakthrough Collaborative is to serve all
students who are passionate about their education and who
qualify for the program.

This program partners with, and serves as a collaborate
network to twenty-four affiliates throughout the country. The
twenty-four affiliates located in individual cities work with
the program to deliver *direct services* to students by offering an
academically challenging environment, which includes after-
school tutoring; mentoring; weekend enrichment programs;
six-week summer programs; test preparation for seventh,
eighth, and ninth graders; and financial aid counseling for both
students and their families.

The twenty-four affiliates are supported by the Breakthrough Collaborative team and operate dependently in

offering these services to middle and high school students; however, the affiliates are independently structured to respond to the needs of their own communities. Therefore, the affiliates offer steps to ensure a rigorous program intended to address the student's social-emotional and academic growth, leading to preparation for preparatory high schools as well as admissions to top colleges throughout the United States.

The following is a list of the twenty-four affiliate cities: Atlanta, Georgia; Austin Texas; Birmingham, Alabama; Boston, Massachusetts; Cincinnati, Ohio; Englewood, Colorado; Fort Worth, Texas; Houston, Texas; Manchester, New Hampshire; Miami, Florida; Minneapolis, Minnesota; New Orleans, Louisiana; New York, New York; Norfolk, Virginia; Philadelphia, Pennsylvania; Pittsburgh, Pennsylvania; Providence, Rhode Island; Sacramento, California; San Francisco, California (2 sites); (Silicon Valley) San Jose, California; San Juan Capistrano, California; Santa Fe, New Mexico; and St. Paul, Minnesota.

Many of the twenty-four sites are *independent private schools*— listed are a few examples of those that partner with the Collaborative: Cincinnati Day School, the Wheeler School, Santa Fe Preparatory, San Francisco Day School, and Norfolk Academy.

The Breakthrough Collaborative website provides a map for you to find your local affiliate site or affiliate school. For more information, please visit: breakthroughcollaborative.org or call (415) 442-0600.

It should be noted that, in addition to the highly supportive education offered to students, the Breakthrough Fellowship program is also committed to training and mentoring future educators.

HELP WITH TESTING

Educational Records Bureau

The Educational Records Bureau (ERB) is a nonprofit organization that oversees the administration, development, and scoring of tests for admissions to independent private schools and select public schools.

Founded in 1927, the ERB is headquartered in New York City and works with 2,000-plus independent and public school members globally. While the primary focus of the organization is to administer and oversee testing for students, ERB is also instrumental in highlighting trends of achievement for its member schools.

The ERB provides a battery of tests designed for admissions to schools for grades two through twelve. The ISEE entrance exam provides a comprehensive picture and insight into a student's strengths, growth, and unique potential for the varying grades. The test material is also designed to assess a student's abilities, and the test changes based on the student's grade level. Regardless of the grade level, the ISEE test covers reading comprehension, mathematics, and verbal and quantitative reasoning. The questions are multiple choice, and the test time is about two hours and fifty minutes, depending on the grade. The cost of the test is approximately $225.

Because the ERB discontinued the Admissions Assessment for Beginning Learners (AABL) tests for the younger children, kindergarten and first grade, individual independent schools are now equipped to administer their own developmental assessment tests. These tests usually measure a young child's intellectual ability, which includes kindergarten and first-grade readiness, verbal and quantitative reasoning, and early literacy. Please consult with the admissions department of your school of interest for more information on their test procedures.

For ISEE testing times, dates, and information on the Educational Records Bureau, please visit erblearn.org or call (1-800) 989-3721.

When to Start the Process

It is advisable to start the process in the spring or fall before the year in which the parent wishes to enroll their child. Also, parents should consider a number of schools, as many schools have more applicants than spaces available for new students. Your first step is *research!* You should begin collecting information about the schools you are interested in at least a year prior to intended enrollment. To do so, call and request a brochure and an application or visit the school's website using the "Find a School" tool or the "Member School Directory." You will find these on the aforementioned organizations' websites.

Further, if given the opportunity to attend school fairs, you can pick up brochures and have a wealth of information available in one location.

You should also spend time assessing your child's attributes, needs, and desires. Some examples to consider are:

- Would your child do best in a single sex or coed environment?
- Does your child require a strong supportive academic setting or are they able to work more independently?
- Would your child do well in a highly competitive environment?

These are just a few questions you should ask yourself. Also, what about you?

- Do you have financial or transportation concerns?
- Are you able to accommodate extended hours, such as with an after-school study hall?
- Do you or your spouse have the time to devote to visiting and applying to schools?

Answering these questions (and more) will help to narrow your decision process.

You will want to schedule a visit to the schools you are considering. This step will help you get a better feel for the schools' environments. While there, as you observe, listen to what your gut is telling you. Also, if your son or daughter is asked to accompany you on the visit, listen to their observations. Ask them questions to get a feel for their impression of the school as well.

Help with Applications

Keep in mind that all schools have varying application processes, fees, and due dates. Make certain you adhere to the due-date deadlines. The earlier you get your application in, the better the chances that it will be reviewed quickly and you will be able to schedule an assessment date of your choosing. Also, remember the admissions personnel are there to assist you, so, if you have any questions or concerns, you should not hesitate to reach out to them.

Financial Aid Information

As mentioned throughout the book, a lot of independent private schools have sought to diversify their school populations, including in terms of socioeconomic diversity. Many parents dismiss the idea of an independent school education for fear of the cost. Yes, some schools cost more simply because of location. Boarding school costs, for example, are higher because they cost more to operate. Bear in mind, schools offer a variety of payment options, including loans, payment plans, or grants—whether partial or full. Grant monies need not be repaid. Many decisions involving finances depend on the family's circumstances, with most schools using a sliding scale. You may think you won't qualify because your family's annual income is $150,000; however, you may qualify for *some* aid. Do not dismiss applying. I cannot stress strongly enough that the schools are more than willing to work with the families in this regard. Many schools have fairly large endowments with monies earmarked specifically for financial assistance.

Regardless of the financial options available to you, make certain all paperwork is handled in a timely manner and submitted within the deadline. Also, whether you go through this entire process on your own or through a supportive program, be sure to keep excellent records and properly dated notes throughout.

BIBLIOGRAPHY

Maeroff, Gene I. , *Don't Blame The Kids*: *The trouble with America's Public Schools* (New York: Mc Graw Hill Book Company, 1982, Epilogue Pg. 235

Dr. Steve Perry, *CNN Anderson Cooper 360 Degrees, Aired October 1, 2009*

Johnson, Stuart, *St. Bernard's Semi-Annual Newsletter*: *Head of School Notes*, Spring June 1994

Roach, Tad, *St. Andrew's School Magazine: An Education For Life*, Head of School's Message, Winter 2005

Andersen, Karen, *Gifted Children: So Intelligent, But They Struggle* Self-Publisher, 2018, Pg 20- Audio Book- Amazon

Wayning, Angela, *Giftedness: Learning How to Recognize and Handle Overexcited Kids with Brains*, Self-Publisher-, 2020. Pg 37, Kindle- Amazon

ABOUT THE AUTHOR

Sharon R. Young is a native New Yorker who was born in Harlem and later moved to the Bronx and Westchester. She holds a BA in sociology from Lehman College of the City University of New York and is currently a licensed health insurance broker in the state of Georgia. For several years, Sharon was a director for a nonprofit agency in the Bronx, providing services to youth and the elderly. She is a strong advocate for educators and education, serving as a teacher and an admissions officer for a local college and a media trade school. She is highly committed to imparting pertinent information about independent private schools to both parents/grandparents and the general public. Semi-retired, Sharon splits her time between her home in Middle Georgia and New York City.